There's No Accounting for the Strangeness of Things

a memoir by
Valley Haggard

Issue 5 —— 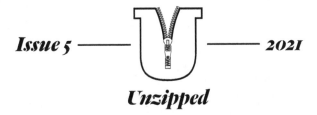 —— *2021*

Unzipped

There's No Accounting for the Strangeness of Things

First published in 2021 by
Life in 10 Minutes Press
Richmond, VA

lifein10minutes.com/press

Distributed by IngramSpark
& Life in 10 Minutes Press

ISBN 978-1-949246-15-5

Printed in the United States of America

First Printing, 2021

About *Life in 10 Minutes*

Life in 10 Minutes is a community of writers sharing stories that are brave and true through classes, workshops, retreats, Zoom, and our online lit mag. Visit **lifein10minutes.com** to read deep, strange, hilarious, heartbreaking, and powerful stories written 10 minutes at a time, and share yours, too!

Homegrown in Richmond, Virginia, *Life in 10 Minutes Press* began with the mission to give passage to books we believe in. We seek to bring readers titles that are brave, beautiful, raw, heartfelt, and vital, and to nurture authors in their publishing journeys.

Learn more at **lifein10minutes.com/press.**

Our mission: We are especially passionate about memoir by women and under-represented voices, nonfiction that challenges the status quo, and boundary-breaking books of all genres. All works published with Life in 10 Minutes Press *are carefully chosen to support our mission and reflect our commitment to promoting fresh, engaging, high-quality storytelling.*

Welcome to *Unzipped*

Life in 10 Minutes fosters love of the immediate. Of the present. The truth. As close up as we can possibly get. *At Life in 10 Minutes,* we reveal life in this moment, right here, right now. Feelings and memories rise from our bodies and spill onto the page. Our stories have curled into knots in our stomachs, fists squeezed around our hearts, pressure against our lungs. We allow these stories to unfurl in our notebooks, releasing us from their grip. As we write, we heal ourselves. As we share our stories, we heal each other. As we heal each other, we heal the world.

Never before has healing the world felt more urgent than now. Now, when connection is more tenuous and precious than ever. When truth is on the chopping block. When the world is on literal and metaphorical fire, when unhealed family and systemic and global trauma threatens to pull us into our most base and destructive selves.

Writing and sharing and reading our stories allows us to process the past, ground in the present and move into the future, freer and more deeply woven into the life-giving, rich fabric of human life. When we write unzipped, we reveal the naked truth, the maskless selves, the vulnerable core. When we write unzipped, we join a community of other writers who agree to hold each other's stories and bear witness, to listen, to believe. To create space for the sacred and profane to exist together on the page.

Punctuation is not our first priority. You might find minor errors. You might see a mistake on the page. Sometimes the writing will reflect the chaotic messiness of urgency. We decided that getting the work out there was more important than getting everything perfect.

This quarterly will share the work of writers who have allowed their truth, their trauma, their pain and struggle, their infinite beauty and whispers of hope to breathe life on the page. We are so excited to share them with you.

With love,
Dr. Cindy Cunningham and Valley Haggard, Co-Editors
Llewellyn Hensley, Graphic Designer
Nadia Bukach, Director of Operations

Looking for past issues of *Unzipped?*

If you missed past issues, they are available for order on the *Unzipped* website.

Issue 1, *Wild Woman*, by Cindy Cunningham

Issue 2, *She Lives Here*, by Kristina Hamlett

Issue 3, *Unraveled Intimacies*, Paula Gillison, Lisa Loving, Mary Jo McLauglin, Sema Wray,

Issue 4, *Inheritance*, by David Gerson and Stephen McMaster,

Issue 6, forthcoming in Spring 2022, will be an anthology of urgent, brave, and true pieces written by a wide variety of writers from the Life in 10 Minutes community. Stay tuned!

— *Life in 10 Minutes Press*

About the press:

Homegrown in Richmond, VA, Life in 10 Minutes Press seeks to give passage to brave, beautiful, raw, heartfelt, and vital works as we nurture writers in their publishing journey.

Learn more at *lifein10minutes.com/press.*

Mission: We are especially passionate about memoir by women and under-represented voices, nonfiction that challenges the status quo, and boundary-breaking books of all genres. All works published with Life in 10 Minutes Press are chosen carefully to support our mission and reflect our commitment to promoting fresh, engaging, high-quality storytelling.

Life in 10 Minutes is a community of writers sharing stories that are brave and true through classes, workshops, retreats, Zoom, and our online lit mag. Visit **lifein10minutes.com** to read deep, strange, hilarious, heartbreaking, and powerful stories written 10 minutes at a time, and share yours, too!

Contents

Introduction

I have been attempting to write a memoir my entire life. My early scribbles, poems, and diary entries were a child's attempt to make sense of her inner world, to untangle the complicated feelings and experiences rising up from within. [*I will love you more than you will love me*, age 4; *Is pain the presence or the absence of love?* age 16].

In high school and college, my short stories and flash fiction were memoir dressed up in clothing you could see straight through. The two handbooks I've written, *The Halfway House for Writers* and *Surrender Your Weapons: Writing to Heal*, have many personal stories, but they are also writing manuals, pulling the reader out of the narrative and onto their own blank page.

All of my previous attempts to fashion a memoir out of the gazillions of ten-minute pieces written in my classes since 2010 felt jagged and incomplete. A skeleton missing too many bones. Then during quarantine in 2020, I pulled my journals out once again, uncovering thousands of pages of handwritten scrawl stuffed into 50+ college-ruled spiral-bound 5 section notebooks. Drowning in the too-much-ness of the task, I called my good friend, Cindy

Cunningham. Cindy is one of the best writers and fastest, most detailed editors I've met in my life and therefore the only person I could imagine pulling me up out of the quicksand of words I found myself drowning in. She was the only person of whom I could make this impossible request.

Would she read through my journals and help me find the entries that held the potential for a larger piece of work? Dear reader, she said yes. Cindy immediately embarked on the arduous task of flagging my work and I am forever grateful for that.

And then the transcription process began. Through a combination of typing, voice to text, and cut + paste, I amassed over 170,000 words of single-spaced material. With the help of my brilliant friend and student, Emily Gambone, I spent weeks churning through the pages, arranging and rearranging, cutting and pasting, editing, writing, rewriting, and trying endless combinations of structures to make sense of the jumbled piles of life. I revisited several of the stories I'd published before, but now in the context of a bigger picture.

After my father's death in July 2020, a path through the twisted forest of plot line and structure became strikingly clear. I could at last see the essence of the story I most needed to tell. I started cutting and within a few hours I had shed a hundred thousand words, cutting my manuscript by more than half. I could finally decipher the lines on the map leading to an ancient and universal story buried beneath the mountains of mud and dirt. The story of a little girl who must learn to love herself and heal her childhood wounds before she is able to become the woman she wants to be with a family of her own.

Acknowledgments

I would like to start by thanking the hard working, badass team of women at Life in 10 Minutes Press who perform the magic trick of making dreams transform into books at least once every quarter: Nadia Bukach the goddess of time management and spreadsheets, Llewellyn Hensley, graphic design maven extraordinaire, and Cindy Cunningham, an editor and writer as vast and beautiful as the ocean.

Thank you to Tim McCready and Emily Gambone both being wonderful friends, and for editing my typos and grammatical errors into submission.

Thank you to the community of writers and students and readers at *Life in 10 Minutes* who are willing to throw themselves over the Cliffs of Vulnerability over and over again. You have all helped the kind of sacred space in which our truest selves and our deepest writing can thrive.

Thank you to my husband Stan who was brave enough to marry a writer, and who, when I asked if I could write our story, said, *yes, and don't leave anything out.*

Thank you to my son, the writer, activist, and musician, Henry Elijah Sterling Haggard, who has already surpassed my wildest dreams in all categories, including handsomeness, intelligence, humor, integrity, wit, and appetite.

Thank you to my mother, Jennifer Yane, who has always believed in me as a writer, and who by her own incredible and lifelong example as a self employed artist showed me that money and security are highly overrated.

To my bonus parents, Donna Haggard, Raymond Buddy Hensley, and Mary Pierce Halsted who've added so much joy and love to my life. Mary, thank you for taking care of all the paperwork in advance of our joining you in what I know is a clean and gorgeous place in heaven.

Thank you to my Dad, who I'm quite sure right now is hanging out with all of the animals, listening to music, making art, and eating pie on a mountain top in the sky.

Dedication

To my father, David Smith, who taught me that there's no accounting for the strangeness of things.

––––––––––

Only part of us is sane: only part of us loves pleasure and the longer day of happiness, wants to live to our nineties and die in peace, in a house that we built, that shall shelter those who come after us. The other half of us is nearly mad. It prefers the disagreeable to the agreeable, loves pain and its darker night despair, and wants to die in a catastrophe that will set back life to its beginnings and leave nothing of our house save its blackened foundations.

—Rebecca West

Jennifer (age 22) and David (age 19) on their wedding day, 1969.

Jennifer and David a few years later, 1973.

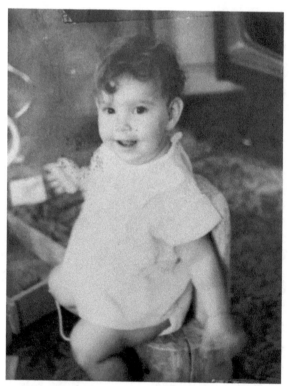

Little Valley, 1977.

David, Valley (age 5) and the Blue Ford Pickup,
1980.

David, 1995.

Valley (age 19), 1995.

Book 1

A Literary Copy of the Great Metaphor

A Literary Copy of the Great Metaphor

My Dad told me that before I was born he quit his job on a whim one day and set out for California in a VW bus with a few jugs of wine and a couple of friends, and that he has always had a thing for drugs and women.

He told me this was his own *literary copy of the great metaphor.*

The Valley

I was conceived in a tent in the Shenandoah Valley on my mother's birthday. I love being named after a place. The Shadow of the Valley of Death. The Valley of the Dolls.

One more cup of coffee before I go / to the valley below, (Bob Dylan)

Val-Pak

Valleydale Wieners, Valleydale Sausage.

Back Alley Valley.

Valley.

When I'm Born

When I'm born my Dad sees himself shoot into outer space, far past the moon. He watches as a meteor soars past him to the earth and as it crashes he hears me cry, my head shooting through my mother's legs, hooked into the stirrups. He can't sleep for days so he stays up drawing my birth announcement and getting high with the neighbors.

Adam and Eve

My mother paints a giant mural of Adam and Eve and their tribe of animals on the wall in my room above my crib. I love the lion the most and maybe that's why I dream they are roaming our neighborhood, prowling, wild, loose.

We always have a small army of cats and my parents nurse an injured seagull back to health in our shed. They name the seagull HeShe. HeShe hops around with me before taking off at last into the clear blank sky.

When I am a toddler, my mother sets up a low hanging clothesline for me in the backyard so I can hang my clothes to dry as she hangs hers. And she gives me a dishpan of hot soapy water on the floor in the kitchen so I can wash my own play dishes. We don't have a television. We dig red clay out of the backyard with our own hands, firing pots and bowls in the oven. We make Shrinky Dinks and I dance with my doll with straps on her feet. My pictures of princesses and cats and little girls cover the walls.

One day when my mother lies in bed crying because we are broke and the toilet has overflowed into the living room, I tell her a magic fish will come and make everything OK. The magic fish and I walk her through the house showing her all of the miracles, the sun through the open window, the meowing cats, the beautiful art she's made, the mural on my wall.

Adam and Eve are guardian angels watching over us, but in my origin story, Adam leaves the garden alone. My mother always said she knew I'd have to take the world apart before I could put it back together again. Like her mother before her, my mother was not interested in housekeeping. Dishes, laundry, and trash piled up. Sometimes we ate dinner on a picnic blanket on the floor when there was no room on the table. My mother valued creativity over cleanliness.

Firecracker

The photographer at my parents' wedding left the lens cap on the camera so the only snapshots of my Mom and Dad as bride and groom were taken by a 7 year-old boy from a vantage point quite close to the floor. My Mom and Dad are both stunning, dramatic, and, to me, could have been movie stars. My mother looks exotic with her cat-shaped eyes, her updo and cupid bow lips. My Dad is tall and swashbuckling and only 19 years old.

A few years after their wedding they will both start dating other people. My Dad will move in with a woman and a man will move in with Mom. One night at a dance in a sudden flash, my mother will know she wants to have a baby and she will tell my Dad to come home now and he will and they will go to the valley and make me. He will leave again, this time for good, two years later.

After that, my Mom, whose own Mom has just died, goes into rages. She has unbearable period cramps. I'm little and I need too much. She is all alone. She scares me when she screams. I scream and cry back. We are firecrackers lighting each other's fuses.

In an amends letter she gives me when I am a mother myself, she explains how she once told me to go to my room, lock the door, and call 911 if she became violent. Eventually, she sought help from a family services center. She told them she was afraid of what she might do. She never hit me, but her mood was my thermometer and when she got hot, my insides felt the fire.

The Little Lady
with the Big Baby

My mother is a black-haired, dark-eyed, olive-skinned beauty but she hates herself because she feels fat. Strangers ask if she is Mexican, Chinese, a gypsy. They say she is exotic. She has tiny hands and feet and she's over a foot shorter than my Dad who towers above her.

I am big and fat and healthy with many rolls. My Mom's friends call us the *Little Lady with the Big Baby*. Mom molds clay sculptures of me lying across her naked belly, nursing. Until I am two, my Mom smokes. Instead of holding her hand, I hold locks of her long black hair as I nurse. Rubbing the nubby ends of her hair between my fingers is my comfort and stability. I sleep between my Mom and Dad in their queen-sized bed with all of my dolls piled up around me. When my Mom and Dad wake up feeling hungover with foul-smelling mouths, they are delighted and amazed at my milk-sweet breath. I babble happily and loudly between them.

When my Dad leaves for good, I'm two and a half. I roam around the house looking for Daze. Daze? Daze? I look for him and I cry but he doesn't answer so my mother puts up photos of him on the walls to try to fill the void. When I'm four and my mother is diagnosed with thyroid cancer and has to stay in the hospital for a week, she takes me to stay with my Dad. Now I can no longer nurse and I am so angry at my mother for leaving, I take all of my art down off the walls.

My Angels

When I'm 2, my Mom starts going to Al-Anon and then AA. I'm the little kid you see sitting on the floor in the back of the smoky AA room, surrounded by books and dolls and markers. My Mom wants to go back to school to study art education but she doesn't know what preschool she should send me to. The ladies at AA tell her to pray about it. *How do I do that?* she asks.

Get quiet and imagine talking to a higher power, they tell her. That night she imagines a hot young guy named Judah holding her tight. In the morning, I sit up next to her in bed and say, Mommy! *My angels were with me last night!*

That week my Mom wins two scholarships to study at VCU. She enrolls me at the VCU children's co-op and she goes to art school.

Longing

When I'm four, my Dad dreams that I'm from Atlantis and he's so shocked he falls backward out of his chair. I dream of lions in my front yard and am afraid to go outside for months. To me, both of these dreams are true. I'm from another world and there's beauty and danger everywhere.

I feel like a shooting star in my Dad's solar system more than a planet or a daughter. A special guest star more than a child with needs and fears and desires. But I never doubt his love for me. Not even when loving him feels more like longing.

***

Sometimes I sleep in a sleeping bag next to his bed, sometimes in a loft he's built in one of the bigger rooms we've lived in; sometimes I have a room of my own. One day after school, my Dad picks me up and says, *Surprise! We've moved!* and he leads me down the hall past our old apartment on Grace Street to a new apartment in the same building, farther down.

He moves every year, but no matter where we go he puts me to sleep with Uncle Wiggly stories, and in the morning wakes me up with the Pachelbel Canon on the record player, and a hot mug of Children's Coffee: warmed milk, honey, and a tablespoon of Folgers.

Sometimes I miss the apartments or townhouses or rentals we leave behind, but in memory, they're just a blur of rooftops and fences and walls and shafts of light and shadow falling through windows onto the floor.

Miracle

When I am 5, Santa brings me a gingerbread house. I sneak into the living room before the sun comes up and gape at the incredible miracle before me. A gingerbread palace perfectly slathered in brilliant white icing, encrusted with enticing rainbows of candied jewels.

I'm not allowed to have sugar and because we are Jewish my mother isn't too crazy about celebrating Christmas, so I cannot fathom my good fortune; that gingerbread house may as well be God herself, it makes me feel more chosen than all of the other Jewish kids combined. My Dad has left, my mother's mother has died and my mother is still getting sober. We live on food stamps and my clothes are from the thrift store. Sometimes the lights are shut off but the gingerbread house makes me feel enormously rich and like I can belong in its sweet, sweet center.

I love it far too much to eat it and preserve it in my room like a shrine.

Over time the cats use it as a litter box and it slowly rots away.

Marry Me

I am in love with my Dad and I ask him to marry me when we are in the checkout line at Safeway. I want to be both his little girl and his wife at the same time.

I remember all his girlfriends, how they sat in the cab of the truck, slept in his bed, determined the color of lights on the tree. I remember knocking on their bedroom door, scared of robbers, no one answering.

I remember the sudden weddings, the sudden apartments, moving suddenly.

I remember finding out my first stepmother, Carrie, left my Dad for a woman.

I remember the African mask Carrie sent me for my high school graduation, long after she'd left my Dad. Now it hangs on my wall, eyes slit, mouth gaping, hungry and blind and beautiful.

I remember at my wedding Carrie looked like an old woman, a cushion of white hair stationed around her head, crinkles at her cheeks and eyes, the saucepot gone, the movie star lost.

I remember when my Dad told me she tried to strangle him in the middle of the night because she felt like he loved me more than her.

I remember when Carrie told me Dad would always be the great love of her life.

Fantastic Secret Lives

In second grade I wear thrift store clothes and have no discernable haircut. School is terrifying and my Dad is the prince who swoops in on his stallion—a Ford 150—to take me to fantasy land. His truck smells like cigarette smoke, sawdust, and plain chapstick from the black and white tube.

We speak to each other as characters in different voices. He is Snorky and I am Little Pig. We call my stepmother Baby. She doesn't play along but we don't care. Our world is all our own. The pets have secret lives, the people walking down the street are aliens, magicians, witches. We make up stories about everything.

My Mom is worried that Dad's make-believe world will make me confused about reality but I don't mind. I like the make-believe world much better. There are monsters and princesses and talking animals and magic. In this world, I can be anybody and anything I want. In this world, a little girl could marry her dad.

Just the Two of Us

Dad and I are locked out of our apartment so we hitchhike to another apartment to pick up a spare key. The man who picks us up chastises my father for hitchhiking with a little girl.

For each apartment, downtown, southside, the fan, near the train tracks on the river, townhouses with pools, sublets on Grace Street, there is a new girlfriend or wife.

Susan is a photographer who wears a beret. Linda is a carpenter and vegetarian who drinks beer. Carrie is a family therapist who teaches me not to say *I know* after receiving a compliment.

Carrie is the most beautiful of them all and the one my Dad marries out in the country by a lake filled with tadpoles. I wear blue gingham and watch the man I love giving himself away to a far more beautiful and sophisticated older woman.

Carrie and my Dad spend a lot of time behind locked doors smoking pot in a loft my Dad builds in an apartment on Auburn Avenue and soon after my Mom finds out, I only get to see him on Wednesday evenings and Sunday afternoons.

I long for him all the rest of the week. My Dad and stepmom have both relapsed and both gone to rehab, but in the end, only my Dad comes home. When I am 10, Dad takes me to a townhouse with tennis courts and a pool and says *this is where we live now, just the two of us.* The swimming pool is bluer than Carrie's eyes. I am glad. I want him to myself in those few short hours a week I can have him at all.

Grandma Billie

My Dad doesn't have a religion, but his Mom, Grandma Billie, loves Jesus. She talks to Jesus, prays with him and sees him on her basement stairs. As much as she loves Jesus, she is never convinced he loves her. When I visit her at Our Lady of Lourdes in Charlottesville we pray together in the chapel and she tells me that at 87 she still doesn't feel good enough for God.

When she was a little girl, my grandma's older sister burned to death in the backyard playhouse and after that, she was never good enough for her grieving mother. Her mother made my grandma dress up in her dead sister's clothes on her dead sister's birthday. My grandma became a nurse and teaches me how to fold hospital corner sheets. She teaches me how to set the table and dress like a girl and act proper and nice.

My grandma gives me a trilogy of action-adventure *Jews for Jesus* romance novels in a bid to bridge the gap between our religions. I love these novels and I love my grandma but I don't know about this Jesus who torments her so much.

My grandma was in and out of mental institutions with electroshock therapy most of her life but you'd never have known from her perfect house and perfect hair and perfect looking life. I never did.

Counter Culture

In the grocery store, my mother swipes a couple of walnuts in the shell from the produce rack, smashes them on the floor with the heel of her boot and digs out meat with her fingers while I hide in the next aisle over. We don't have a television until I am 13 because my mother wants to nurture my creativity, and then when we get one my mother insists I keep it in my room so she doesn't have to see it or hear it at all.

My mother is not big on housework and once I embarrass her by asking a neighbor what an iron is. Sometimes our cat sleeps in the drying rack while dishes pile up in the sink and we eat dinner on a picnic blanket on the floor because the dining room table is too crowded. We shop at yard sales and thrift stores but my Mom always seems to scrape together enough money when we really need it.

We go to free festivals and art shows and exhibits and one time she panhandles at the Virginia Museum lobby to buy an ice cream cone for me after we look at the art. At home we read Shakespeare and Ionesco, dividing up the roles and characters between us. She sometimes splurges on theatre so that I will become cultured. Once, when we are 11, she convinces my cousin and me to go with her to a play at VCU, the local college, instead of the movies. She is horrified when the actors perform simulated fellatio on stage, but my cousin and I conclude that culture is important after all.

My mother grew up comfortably middle class but rejected the life of a teacher her Dad wanted for her, becoming an artist like her mother instead, but without a partner or steady income. My mother's mother threw away little and did housework less, and my mother followed in her footsteps. My Mom's Dad was angry all the time and yelled at his family the way my mother would come to yell at me. The difference is, I was allowed to yell back.

Kenny

Recently my Mom and I went through a box of her old photos and I saw a photograph of her and Kenny, her boyfriend who was in prison when they were still together. They both look young and beautiful and vibrant on the other side of the brown Kodachrome. My mother was friends with another man named Kenny once, but he had a blonde mustache and was a lion-trainer and she only saw him once every three years, when the circus came to town.

Prison Kenny and my Mom met when he called her to ask about ordering some of her buttons for his mother. They got to talking and eventually, she decided to meet him during visiting hours. This became a regular occurrence and a couple of times she brought me, too. Kenny was gentle and soft-spoken with dark brown skin and a soft short Afro.

My Mom said Kenny's wife cut off his dreadlocks in his sleep the night before he went to prison just like Sampson and Delilah, that he'd been a barber, that he had been framed for his crime, that he was innocent. Once Kenny sent me a chocolate pecan log and letters about jail inside of envelopes with elaborate drawings of tigers. I liked Kenny, was never scared of Kenny, and never questioned why my mother brought such a kind and gentle man into our lives.

What We Do

I read. I read all the time. Seven, eight books a week. I tell my mother that when I grow up I want to be a famous reader. We don't have a TV. We have books. We have art supplies and poetry and plays and the red clay we dig up from our backyard and bake in the oven. I don't have brothers or sisters. I read and read and read. My Mom serves kale and brown rice and tofu and quinoa and everything she bakes seems to have raisins.

When I'm at my Dad's apartment we watch TV. We watch Knight Rider, Buck Rogers, the A-Team, and The Wild Wild West. We eat TV dinners and cheeseburgers and pepperoni pizza and milkshakes. He gets cable and we watch MTV and VH1. I dress up like Madonna and sing her songs and form a Madonna cover band with my girlfriends. Dad takes me to the movies and out to eat. I get to order whatever I want.

One of my counselors says the first man I ever dated was my Dad.

Bad

I say everything bad to my mother. I let it rip. She gets all of it. We talk, scream, curse, beat our chests, calm down, make up, evaluate, apologize, forgive, ask forgiveness.

I hold nothing back from my mother except what I am lying to her about—sneaking out, drinking, having sex, smoking. Those things are not talked about until she finds them out and then the shit hits the fan. But then we talk. Luckily my mother has a therapist to talk to as well. A bearded Jewish man named Peter.

My mother says from the day I became a teenager, Peter helped raise me.

I never complain to my Dad. I never beg or tell him how much I miss him or that not living with him makes me sad. In his presence, I soak up the love that is there. I don't let my badness show. I save all of that for my mother.

Beautiful

My parents are both ravenous but for different things. My mother eats steamed kale and rice cakes and jiggly bricks of tofu and celery sticks a foot-long. She doesn't eat sugar because her mother died of diabetes—her toes, and then one leg amputated before her early death at 68. My Dad eats cheeseburgers and pizza and chocolate shakes and lets me choose between frosted donuts and bubblegum ice cream for dessert.

I bounce back and forth between them on my scheduled visits, always hungry for what I don't have. A mother or a father, a dessert, or a home-cooked meal. I am the one constant in both of their lives and I'd like to be everything to both of them---partner, child, lover, friend, spouse, daughter, queen.

My mother looks in the mirror and says *I'm fat* and then finds another diet or lifestyle food plan while telling me I am beautiful just the way I am. I don't believe her. I want to cut the fat off my thighs.

I long for my Dad to come pick me up and take me to Wendy's and Baskin-Robbins and pizza at the mall so I can feel loved and full and special. My Dad tells me I'm smart and kind but never that I'm pretty. When we play pick-up sticks, he tells me my hands are so steady I could be a surgeon. But what I want, more than anything, is to be beautiful.

Good Citizen

My Mom doesn't want me going to school with all white kids in the county so she sends me to a school in the city with mostly Black kids. Sarah is in my Kindergarten class, half white, half Dominican, and the only other kid as nerdy as me.

When the teacher leaves the room, she puts me in charge of the class —I have after all won the Good Citizenship award for the school. Every time I am left in charge I write Sarah's name on the blackboard in white chalk because she is the only kid in the class I know won't beat me up. At Bellevue, there are plenty of beatings. Girls beat other girls, boys pinch girls, and the teachers beat and pinch the boys in the closet until their brown skin turns dark red.

Sarah has to write *I will not talk in class* 100 times but she is still nice to me, I still go to her house some days after school; I am still invited to her birthday parties. At lunch, I sit with Rashida and Regina whom they call Regina Vagina. I love Regina because she gives me her pink Hostess snowballs while my Mom packs me tofu and celery and carob bars, lunches so embarrassing I keep the lid to my lunchbox shut as tight as I can.

After lunch, we line up in the hall before going back to our class and girls threaten to beat me upside the head if I am wearing dirty clothes or the same outfit as the day before. Sarah and I get a notebook to keep track. I have a crush on Kenneth, the fat boy in class because he is so nice and doesn't accuse me of starting slavery, like some of the other kids.

At recess, I don't like being chased and pinched by boys so l stand against the brick wall of the building getting cobwebs in my hair.

County School

When I am in the third grade my Mom comes to pick me up from school early and sees me swinging a silver whistle on a chain on the playground to keep the other kids at bay.

For fourth grade, I am back in the county school in a class of 9-year-olds who play sports and are already going steady. I have a crush on Jay, a jock with blonde hair and blue eyes who is the boyfriend of Lindsay and has no idea I am alive. My lunches from home are still embarrassing and I love the days I can buy a tray of pizza and tater tots with my reduced lunch ticket so for 20 minutes my food and I seem normal.

I am put in the Talented and Gifted group and make straight As but never feel like I fit in with these kids who seem to have lots of money and big houses and both parents, and who've been in school with each other since Kindergarten.

Instead, I stay in touch with Sarah, spending the night at her house or having her spend the night at mine. I am the only kid in the fourth grade who doesn't vote for Ronald Reagan in the mock election.

When my Mom comes in to give a presentation about Hanukkah, my differences are further amplified, an outlier at Christmas time when all the Christian festivities are at their apex. Because she played softball when she was young, my mother makes me join a little league softball team called the Hornets. I am terrible at softball but it does make me feel a little bit more like everyone else.

The Fox and the Hound

When my Dad lives in an apartment on Grace Street, we have a neighbor named Patrick. He is a white boy with auburn hair and blue eyes, a few months older than me, and we go to different schools. I only stay with my Dad on Wednesdays and Sundays but all of the windows and doors stay open and I'm free to roam the neighborhood. Dad plays Bob Marley and Bob Dylan, and cats and dogs from the neighborhood wander in the open doors to sit in his lap.

Patrick and I build a teepee out of trash from the alley and race along the cracked jagged sidewalks of Grace Street and for once I feel well-matched because he doesn't always win. One day Patrick tells me there's something in the alley by our fort and he wants me to go with him to see. He points at a dirty bundle of rags next to the dumpster. *It's an abortion,* he tells me.

What's that? I ask.

A *dead baby,* he says and I feel sick and weird and never tell anybody about it, not until I'm writing this now.

A few weeks later when my Dad picks me up from school, he tells me that Patrick's house caught fire and burned down and his family moved away. But he'd dropped off a carefully rendered orange and blue and green paint-by-numbers Fox and the Hound that says *To Valley from Patrick, 1982* on the back in neat lettering with a perfect little heart. Patrick showed me something someone else lost and now he was gone and I was left with a picture. I was seven and even though I was terrified of everyone at school I'd had a friend of my own, even if the things we found together I could never speak of again.

Shedding

When I am nine my Dad sheds his skin. He gets a staph infection from a rusty nail driven into his knee on a carpentry job where he's building a house and spends three weeks in the hospital hallucinating about the evolution of the Shenandoah Valley, a mob of bakers on parade in New York City, and his brother Michael whom he calls the King of Hawaii. He recognizes me some days and others he has no idea who I am at all.

It is strange to see my Dad stripped down, his tall, tan muscled body limp against crisp, antiseptic sheets. When he finally comes home to our townhouse in Southside he recognizes me as his daughter, but his skin has come off in long spindly sheaths like the black snake high in his tree who shed his skin on my wedding day.

Camping

In the summers, Dad takes me camping on his mountain property in Rockingham County. I run through the woods wild for days, never changing out of my nightgown and getting brambles in my tangled hair. I collect fallen branches and logs and sticks and dried leaves to burn. We cook our food on the fire and haul our water up in gallon jugs from the city.

There's a swing that seems to levitate out over the edge of a treacherous cliff. I love to pump my legs hard and feel like I can fly. Nights are freezing cold and I shiver in my sleeping bag until I hear the sound of Dad making the fire.

When it's time to leave the mountain, or if we have to drive into town for supplies, Dad lets me stand up in the bed of the truck holding onto the ladder rails while he bumps down the narrow curvy road as fast as he can. I ride all the way home in the back of the pickup bundled up under blankets and know to be absolutely silent the time he is pulled over for speeding.

If our trip to the mountains is canceled, I turn the AC down as low as I can and pretend to camp in my bedroom, pulling out the sleeping bag and setting up camp on the floor. My Dad carves me bows and arrows, teaches me how to build a fire, how to strike a match.

Mary + Dad

Mary is different from Dad's other girlfriends. There is an unshak-able calm about her and she wears pink nail polish and pink lipstick instead of patchouli and chapstick. She has two sons. Will, 13, who has a mullet, and Matt, 17, who has a mohawk. They both have tattoos.

I'm 12 and wear acid-washed jeans and turquoise eyeliner and have feathered wings in my blob of hair. I'm completely gobsmacked by these two wild and handsome dark-eyed boys who I only meet twice before they become my stepbrothers—both at Little League games—soccer for Will, and softball for me. How will I live with these strangers, when I can barely look them in the eye?

After dating for six months, Mary and Dad get married in Mary's parents' backyard. I wear a bright yellow dress and try to brush my awkward bushy hair into a wave. I am between styles and have no idea what I look like or who I am. Mary looks beautiful in white and my Dad wears suspenders. Matt and Will can barely stay contained in the suits they strip off right after the ceremony, sneaking away to decorate Mary's station wagon with shaving cream and empty coke cans.

Congratulations Mom + David they write on the rear windshield that pulls away from all of us down the road clunking cans and exhaust into the night.

New Constellations

I am an only child until I turn 13 when Dad marries Mary. Suddenly I have two stepbrothers and then Mom marries Buddy and I have two stepsisters and my family becomes a web of marriage and blood and different last names and many houses spread across time and space.

We feel like a magnet attracting magnets, stars rotating around other stars, new constellations forming in our family sky. All of my parents become friends with each other eventually, good friends even, my parents' divorce ancient history. Now my Mom and Buddy help care for my Dad in memory care, picking him up for dinner, to go shopping, to go to AA. My stepsister's mother has started taking my writing class and I have come to love her, too.

And now, everyone is coming to my house tonight to celebrate my child. The fabric of my childhood was ripped apart but sewn back together, stitch by stitch, year by year, and now it is a blanket big enough to cover us all.

Creativity Award

In 8th grade, I receive the school-wide creativity award. My Mom takes me to Hecht's bargain-basement where we choose a shimmery, deep green velvet skirt to wear to the awards ceremony. Earlier in the year, I'd won the creative writing contest in my English class for a story about a cat that reincarnates into a girl and you can tell because they both have the same brilliant blue eyes.

I've also written an essay for a local Teen Zine about breaking the cycle of addiction in my family. How I've learned enough about drugs and alcohol from my parents and I don't want to repeat their mistakes. How I don't want my creativity confused with getting high. I want my imagination to stay pure, untouched by foreign substances. I don't drink in middle school but I do stay up one night with my friend Caroline after eating a box of No-Doze, terrified I am going to die.

I start drinking in high school and it's like my former self, the one that wanted to stay clean and sober to preserve her mind and body and spirit, never existed at all.

Tug of War

The first time I have a beer is at Louise's house after she sings
I *Don't Know How to Love Him*, from *Jesus Christ Superstar* while her
parents are out of town. The beer is gross and tastes like warm
metal and I only drink half, but of course I write about it in the diary
I hand my mother the next week so she can read something else
I have written, an amateur move I'll never make again.

You had a beer? my Mom asks, all of the years of AA and NA and Al-Anon
and Alateen compressed into the deep pitch of her disappointment.
As punishment, she grounds me for a month but this is when she is
square dancing regularly so when she is at a dance I sneak over the
boys she so badly wants to keep out.

I am 13 and this is where our troubles take a new turn. The moth-
er-daughter wars, the push-pull, the screams, the forgiveness, and
the blessings. She tries to keep me in a cage I claw my way straight
through.

When I am 42, my own son and many of my students are 13. And
they are children, tiny babies, so young and so old in that

precarious slanted in between. Maybe the only way to win at tug-of-war is to stop pulling as hard as you can or to drop the rope you never really had control of at all.

Experience Everything

I grow up going to AA and NA conventions around the country with my mother who sells inspirational buttons she makes herself, as part of her business, *Jennifer Unlimited*. We go to conventions in Orlando, Nashville, Dallas, Seattle, Cheyenne, Baltimore, Seattle, New York, San Diego. For a while, I collect photo buttons of myself posing with recovering addicts. I am 12, 13, 14, 15, 16, 17.

They are grizzled, strung out, and long-haired, often toothless. Some have snakes. Some, my mother dates. Some I sneak away with. Many I dance with in big hotel ballrooms with strobe lights and a DJ—everyone stark raving clean and sober.

I am not yet legally old enough to have had my first drink but by 14 I'm already drinking as much as I can. I work the button table with my mother and she pays me in one-dollar bills which I carry around balled up in a sock. Once I lose that sock in Florida and cry through our entire day at Epcot Center, $47 gone, more money than I'd ever had all at once in my life.

I keep a big fold-up map of the US from National Geographic and trace our trips in ballpoint pen — the campsites, the bunkhouses, the Cracker Barrels where we can check out books on tape to return at another Cracker Barrel in another state, the fancy hotels, the recovery slogans, and the men, always the men who come from far away and are hollowed out trying to fill back up and little me who knows only two things for sure and repeats them to my mother again and again.

I won't learn from your mistakes, I'm going to learn from my own, and, I want to experience everything.

Sweet Pink Wine

When I am 14, I have my first taste of Boone's Farm Strawberry Hill at the punk band Johouse downtown. There are boys covered in tattoos, girls wearing spiked dog collars, and Anne is writing runes on the wall. We have a bottle we keep passing back and forth between us. It tastes like Kool-Aid but makes my stomach feel hot and my chest real loose and there's a warm buttery sensation in my throat like words are rising out of my mouth through fizzy water. I love this feeling. It replaces the hollow clanging echo, the opaque untouchable core, like I can feel my insides when before there was nothing at all.

Rosser and I lock ourselves in the water heater closet and he puts his hand between my legs in a place only I've touched myself before. It is sparkly and warm and for those 15 minutes, I don't have to share him with anyone else. He is all mine, blonde dreadlocks, and green eyes and perfect cleft lip and raspy voice, unbroken, untouched, special, close, and beautiful until the next week when I find out he's dating Brittney Adams, a tiny blonde punk who looks like a cheerleader. I can't have Rosser anymore, but I can have more Boone's Farm Strawberry Hill.

My Friends

My friends are the misfit fringe kids from all the high schools in town. We meet at the river, on train tracks, in parks, and in the basements or backyards of our parents. We are bonded by conversations that never cease winding through our days and nights like the river where we swim in the city.

We are creative and brilliant, flunking out of school, reading banned books, creating our own thesis of this fucked up world. The boys call themselves the Nowhere Generation, and the girls make good grades but drink on school nights and weekends. In this group, I meet Carter, about two years older than me and maybe an inch shorter but broad in the chest, and strong as a bull, and with turquoise eyes that look like tropical water.

He writes plays, parodies, and manifestos. He's funny and self-deprecating and I laugh until I cry every time I'm with him. Eventually, we start hanging out alone and I feel safe and loved in his presence. He gives me his black leather jacket and an amber ring and we make out on his parents' couch and in parks all over the city. He comes to all of my family gatherings and calls my Mom *Ma'am* which she hates so they compromise and he calls her *mammy*.

I learn how to drink with Carter and I lose my virginity to Carter and I love him with every part of me that knows how to love.

Young Writers

The summer after my tenth-grade year my Mom sends me to the UVA Young Writers' Workshop, paying for it with money her father, my Grandpa Boris left to her when he died.

As young writers, we live in the dorms, eat our meals at the cafeteria and take workshops with writers and professors who take our work seriously like we are people, not just kids. Carter rides his bike from Richmond to Charlottesville to see me for fifteen minutes and I'm flattered but I also want this new, exotic world of writers all to myself. I am in Utopia. No one thinks I'm weird for the stories I write about Jesus and Manuel Noriega and my father's feet. No one makes fun of the way I dress in vintage dresses or thrift store mumus or overalls and combat boots. Everyone is weird but it is not a competition of weirdness, it is a celebration.

When my Mom comes to pick me up from camp on the last day, I cry harder than I've ever cried in my life.

I go back the next summer and meet a poet named India, one of the camp counselors. She is tall and gangly with eccentric mannerisms and I think she is impossibly cool. When I find out she goes to Sarah Lawrence College in New York, I decide that's where I will go too. It's the only school I apply to and I am accepted early admission.

The summer before I leave for New York, India invites me to her apartment downtown. I feel so lucky, so chosen, so grown up. When she shows me pictures of her naked with both women and men, I am proud that she considers me mature enough to get her like I do. Years later I'll learn that India has died of an overdose on her couch in her apartment and I'll feel a sadness and a strangeness I'm not sure how to name.

After I graduate high school I go back to UVA's Young Writers Workshop where I work as a counselor for two summers. The July I turn 19, my mother picks me up from camp so we can meet my favorite author, Tom Robbins, at a party in Richmond. A woman named the Pygmy Queen had asked my mother to make buttons for their reunion and my mother said she will if we are allowed to attend the reunion, too.

Several people at the party mistake me for Tom Robbins's fifth wife who also has dark hair and green eyes. I am enthralled when I get to speak to Tom Robbins who seems to have snake rings on each one of his fingers. I tell him I'm studying creative writing in college and he says that I should drop out immediately. I'm wasting my time. I should do something useful instead, like go to nursing school. I argue with him, but I'm terrified he's right. When we leave, my mother gives him my stories to read on the plane ride back to Seattle.

Waffle House

When I'm 16, I apply for a job at Waffle House because I think it will be ironic. But the job loses its irony the instant I have to put on an apron with my name embroidered on the lapel and an ugly brown bonnet, that's really a visor. I try to slip it off when Bubba, my manager who's a drug dealer, is in the back, but usually he's watching me through the one-way mirror.

When the phone rings I have to say *Thank you for calling your friendly Waffle House,* a phrase I repeat in my dreams. Mostly I wait on deadbeat dads and the widowed old people of the city who want to look at another human face after they've finished their meal. They leave me a handful of change for tips which I use to buy my birth control pills at the Fan Free Clinic downtown.

Waffle House never closes, but there are some dead zones, like between the lunch and dinner rush. That's when everyone gets stoned in the back. Doris smokes through her tracheotomy and yells at the rest of us to shut the hell up. The job I hate most, next to scrubbing the toilets, is refilling the thirty-five-pound tub of Thousand Island salad dressing, mixing together the chunks of ketchup, relish, and mayo.

Sometimes Carter rides his bike over to visit me, and then I take the visor off whether Bubba is looking or not. Usually, when Carter comes, he tells me stories about his band or what the boys call *Death Games* he's been playing in the woods with our friends where they chase each other with bows and arrows and real fire. Sometimes he brings me a cup full of butterscotch chips from the yogurt shop where he works as I finish the summer serving plates of steaming hashbrowns—scattered, smothered, covered, and chunked.

Back Alley Valley

I buy my first car, a five-speed silver Honda Civic with red fabric interior, for $500. I glue a Barbie in a turquoise bikini with an Anarchy sign on her forehead to the hood.

My Dad has been teaching me how to stick-shift in his truck, the full-size four-wheel-drive we take through the mountains, in my high school parking lot, but it isn't until I have a car of my own and a license from DMV that I really learn how to drive.

Juicy Jessie contributes handfuls of loose change to my gas fund and when my wipers break during a rainstorm she stands up through the sunroof and tells me when to go. We invite boys over that we want to kiss, and drink 40s, and think we're invincible.

I'm Back Alley Valley and together we all pack into my Honda like feral cats, bodies crammed together, exhilarated with the closeness and the freedom, heading to the train tracks or the river or each other's houses or to see bands play in the city, off the radar of our parents who have different lengths for our leashes.

When I leave for Italy at 20, I trade my Honda for a Eurorail ticket. That car is my ticket to the entire world.

Celebration of Womanhood

To say I am hungover is a sad understatement. I've spent the morning throwing up after a night of blacking out. I'd gone to Carter's Jägermeister party and couldn't remember anything after the third shot. I don't remember who drove me home. I do remember being covered in hickeys and hearing that I'd been locked in a bathroom with Carter's best friend, Jason.

My mother sees my first trip to the gynecologist the same way she sees my first period. As a celebration of womanhood. As a ritual to be recognized. She plans a special lunch for us to go to afterward. I am barely coherent when we get in the car to go, not quite done throwing up.

My mother tries to give me the benefit of the doubt. She tries to remain calm. But after the doctor tells her the whole list of things they've tested me for her voice raises a few octaves. *Why did they give you the chlamydia test, Valley? That's only for women who've had sex before.*

I guess because I've had sex before, **Mom,** I say. I am 16 and buying my birth control from the Fan Free Clinic with rolls of nickels, dimes, and quarters I make waitressing. My Mom refuses to eat a bite of her fancy lunch which I can't stomach the sight of either. She asks the waitress to box everything up so we can take it to go.

Buddy

When my Mom meets Buddy on a recovery cruise on the Annabel Lee, he pulls out his harmonica and then quotes Mark Twain while she stands on the darkened bow of the ship and swoons. I am 16 and his girls are six and eleven, and one of the things that make us love Buddy is how he plays Pretty Pretty Princess with them, wearing the clip-on diamond earrings and pearl necklaces and bejeweled tiaras from the set.

I also love Buddy because he takes my mother's focus off of me during my senior year of high school. I am convinced I should be emancipated and living in an apartment downtown instead of in my childhood bedroom. Buddy moves in shortly after I leave for college and there are a million or more times I am grateful to him, providing a calm island in my Mom's wild ocean, becoming a loving and generous and present grandpa to my kid, adept at speaking the foreign language of electricity and wire with my husband. All while being the kind of man who can operate power tools as handily as he can cry and share his true emotions through guitar, harmonica, song, and word.

Trust

Sarah and I are 17-year-old high school seniors when my Mom enrolls us in the J. Sargeant Reynolds Outdoor Adventures community college course. The teacher named Dave is a short man with a white beard who wears turquoise sweatsuits and looks just like Papa Smurf. The class is full of single moms and retirees and we are definitely the only teenagers. We go camping, spelunking, hiking, and canoeing with this motley crew, including Doug who has a mullet and likes to stand between us to call himself *a thorn amongst the roses.*

My bangs catch on fire in the open flame of my headlamp in the blackness of the cave we are belly crawling through, but otherwise, Sarah and I pass the class unscathed and even make Honor Roll at the college.

That same year my Mom hires the two of us to go to a Narcotics Anonymous convention in West Virginia to sell her recovery buttons. By ourselves. In her minivan. We have each just gotten our driver's licenses and have not yet spent much time on the road. But my mother entrusts us with her minivan, her entire business, and our very lives. Sarah and I are already drinking and doing drugs with our friends but given such awesome responsibility, we fly straight.

We set up and take down the booth on time like clockwork. We make photo buttons and sell recovery buttons and keep meticulous track of the money. *Trust the Process, One Day at a Time, First Things First.* We don't sneak out of the lodge in search of alcohol or spend the night with any of the recovering drug addicts. We make more money at that convention than my Mom ever did by herself. My Mom thinks it was our big smiles and boobs, but we think it was our winning personalities.

Poison Ivy

By the second semester of my senior year, my mother lets Carter spend the night with me in my loft. We go to his senior prom in matching purple outfits. He wears purple rasta pants and a top hat and I wear a lavender vintage gown and orange fishnets with combat boots that horrify my Great Aunt Eva who is visiting from New Jersey. We know we won't marry each other, but we swear that one day after we are widowed we will find each other again.

One night, a few months before leaving for college, I get a message from Carter on my answering machine. He is choking back sobs. He has to tell me something. I wait for him in the front yard. When he gets out of his car he stands against the driver's side door, sobbing. He and my best friend got drunk and had sex the night before. She was going to call me too, but he wanted to be first. It feels like a cat is clawing its way out of my chest. Do I make him leave or do I make him stay? Do I call her back or ignore her attempts to apologize? I only remember the friends who take me in, feed me whiskey, play music, and pet my head while I weep.

My mother takes me to a mountain resort with her sponsee, Mona, who is recovering from a boob job and they nurse me like I am a tiny baby. I get poison ivy which burns and spreads and tears my tenderest skin until it's raw and bloody. I knew sex was powerful, I knew it was explosive, but I'd never before experienced it as a weapon that could be turned so violently against me.

Victim Songs

My mother hates it when I listen to the music I love best. Heart-ache, breakups, misery, love is pain and pain is love. *Just kiss my cheek before you leave me, baby.*

Stop listening to those victim songs! she says. But I feel like a victim and I don't know how to transform from the girl tied to the train tracks into the woman who will rescue her.

I don't know how to be the heroine of my own story. If a man doesn't choose me, I am unchosen. If he doesn't love me, I am unloved. If he doesn't call me beautiful, I am ugly. I don't know that it doesn't make a difference if a man wants me and loves me and finds me beautiful because my need has no bottom and no amount of someone else's love will ever keep me filled up.

Greatest Enemy

I have a tiny dorm room covered in velvet Jesus wall hangings and oil paintings by my mother. My Brother Word Processor is stained with coffee and wine and candle wax. My record player plays everything fast and I learn Patsy Cline and Tom Waits and Leonard Cohen that way. There are rows of empty wine, beer, and liquor bottles under my desk. I read Dostoyevsky and Dorothy Parker, Hermann Hesse, and Anna Akhmatova when I'm lonely and even though they elicit sharp laughs and twists inside that hinge on the familiar, they accentuate my loneliness. I'd give all my books for one whistle at my window. The ones who come are not the one I want.

This one sleeps upside down in my bed and in the morning tells me he dreamt of his mother. This one smokes a pipe and wears a crucifix. When I try to kiss him, this one yells *you're all woman!* and runs out my door. This one doesn't talk at all. This one I wish wouldn't. My room is a fishbowl of loneliness. My room is meant to hold me but it hides me deep inside myself instead.

Thomas takes my hair out of the barrette and calls me his greatest enemy. Thomas pretends he doesn't see me when he walks past me on the path through the heartbreaking flowers of spring. Thomas has sex with me without kissing me and then will not look me in my eyes. He will leave in a few months without saying goodbye but he will call every few years when he's drunk and tell me he's sorry and that I'm the measuring stick by which he measures the world. But I don't know this now.

Now when I go home I break up with Carter but sleep with him one last time in an agonizing goodbye. Now I stay up until 4 am drawing hanged women and writing poems about being eclipsed. Now I eat in the cafeteria but can't taste the food. Now I cut my hair without looking in the mirror. Now I drink as much as I can. Now I look everywhere for something, but I am still alone with myself.

Pretty Little Head

The summer my mother takes me to interview for Sarah Lawrence College, I take a week-long memoir writing workshop with Madeleine L' Engle at the Omega Institute in upstate New York. The workshop is for ages 18+ and though I'm 17, my mother encourages me to write to Madeleine L'Engle herself and ask for an exception.

My request is granted and I get to spend a week with my hero and twenty other writers in workshops and critique groups, beginning to tell for the first time the story of my life with my father and his wives.

During my freshman year of college, I submit my work to the school-wide fiction contest. I've written 12 pieces of flash nonfiction and combined them into a collection called *Pretty Little Head*. I show Thomas my stories one afternoon in his dorm room. I have written about Carter and Death Games and the Outdoor Adventures community college class and working at Waffle House and how, when I went home for Thanksgiving break it seemed like my mother was shrinking.

Thomas skims the pages and then looks up at me. *You really need to travel,* he says, his accent polished, his green eyes casual, his blonde hair a shimmery shade of gold.

I'd walked into his room a woman but sitting on his bed I become a stupid little girl.

My stories win first place in the contest and I am awarded a prize by Grace Paley, another writer I love who used to teach at the college, but all I can hear as I accept my award is the echo of Thomas' words in my ear.

New Genre of Love Song

When Edward and I first meet, I wear floor-length dresses, hand-me-downs from the thrift store, ripped-up fishnets, and combat boots. Blonde-haired and golden-skinned, he has the face of a Playgirl, a GQ devil, mischievous and sweet. Will I ever get over how pretty he is? Those cupid bow lips and sea-green eyes and the lean, muscled body of a dancer. He's been a stripper in DC and is a social work major with a minor in dance. He knows New York City and the wilderness around it like different sides of the same hand. He takes me into both, like an adventure guide to explore what draws me in and terrifies me most.

I am a wreck all the time, learning how to smoke and read French poetry, staying up all night crying and pining. He takes me dancing in the city, skinny dipping in gorges, to hear music beautiful enough to make even me want to sing. We sleep chest to chest in the closet he rents, or in my dorm room, smoking and drinking. And then we drive cross country, camping in the Rockies. He lends me his jeans because I've only packed dresses. We climb through Arches and Wind River Valleys, ride Ferris wheels and horses, cook. on fires and sleep under tarps and blankets in the freezing cold and howling wind. We paint constellations on gourds and trace stars with our fingers. We explore the world like hungry, fearless children.

I even sing for him, *summertime and the livin' is easy, catfish are jumping, and the cotton is high,* the wistful bluesy lyrics of *Summertime.*

If I ever married a woman, it would be you and we would have babies, he says, and I am free to love him with my entire heart without being afraid he'll break it. He can talk to anybody, but when we are together, I only want to talk to him.

I absorb him like sound. When I leave New York, I feel like I've left my heart with him.

North Star

I call Jenne my North Star. She has sun-blonde hair and ocean-blue eyes, and even though I am dark and troubled she doesn't feel sorry for me or put me down. She speaks to me as if I am just like her, fearless and full of life. The summer before our senior year, I take a road trip to visit her in her big skyed home state of Colorado, stopping in Opryland and Taos, wearing only vintage dresses and smoking "Gunsmoke" cigarettes along the way. She takes me to the dude ranch where she is a wrangler, working hard and dirty like the cowboys.

We go on a 10 hour pack ride into the mountains to pack out a hunting party. I've never ridden a horse before but she teaches me as we go, redirecting my horse, time and again, to stay the course, following on the path behind her.

I mourn for Jenne when she doesn't come back to New York but instead goes to South America, leaving me to graduate with my depressed friends. I don't know if I can make it another year without her in cold, icy New York where it snows for months and no one else has the sun in their smile like she does. I want Jenne to come and pluck me out of my misery and carry me to her mountaintop where people spent the morning drinking coffee and planning day trips.

She surprises me for my graduation, throwing rocks up at my window, but not before hitchhiking all the way down to Chile, just her and her dog after running a bed a breakfast with an alcoholic monkey in Venezuela. All of her boyfriends were Latino men who liked to watch her dance. She spent days walking through the mountains of Peru, separated from her guide and her horse. And, when she finally came back and was the landlady of her own apartment in Portland, she tracked down and threw out the tenant who shit in the basement.

One night deep in the basement of the costume department at Sarah Lawrence, Jenne hemmed my dirty, ragged ball gown while I wept and wept about my broken heart. When I'm lost, she knows where we should go.

Gorgeous and Forbidden Bouquet

During the first semester of my junior year abroad, I live with a host family deep in the throes of marital strife. I don't understand their meaning, but hear their words fall like bricks outside my room. My room is ice cold but I am allowed to smoke in it. Every morning my host mother comes in and makes my bed whether I want her to or not, while I pour hot espresso into boiled milk and slather apricot jam onto hard, dry Tuscan toast.

I usually don't know where I am going that day or how to get there. I pray to be on the right bus and jump off if I'm not. As lost as I get, as poorly as I can read maps or speak the language, somehow, eventually, I always end up where I need to go. I am desperate for kindness and attention and let middle-aged Italian men I can't talk to buy me coffee.

Every time it rains I find photographs of Italian women in the street or hovering around the gutter, each one different as if they are postcards addressed to me. Every corner is art, every person I meet a mystery I can't understand.

I have never been a great traveler, and I am no longer a good citizen. I steal wine from the gates of a villa the school housed us in. I run out on bar tabs just to see if I can. At a beautiful botanical garden with sculptures and waterfalls and scenes out of Eden, I pick flowers, creating the most gorgeous and forbidden bouquet that the guards confiscate before I am allowed out of the gates. I am selfish and hungry and want everything for my own.

Eventually, I move into an apartment near the train station. Drunk on Chianti and Dante, I name all the rooms I inhabit after the rings of hell. My bedroom is *Traitor to Friends and Family*. My new neighbors fight and yell too, but by this point, I have a better idea of what their words mean, bitter and cruel.

Even the Lives
We Haven't Lived

Gwen and I rent an apartment in Florence above a Chianti shop on a block full of drug dealers and prostitutes. When we leave, we give one of the women our winter coat, but I can no longer remember which one of us it was.

We travel to Amsterdam together, and Budapest and Prague and Vienna and Copenhagen. We ride on trains and buses and ferries and cabs. We see so many men masturbating on different forms of public transportation that we make a game of connect the dots on our map.

We swear if you trace our footsteps you will draw the outline of God's face.

We drink beer in bars and run out on our bar tabs. We buy fresh olives and mozzarella and tomatoes at the market and brew our own espresso until I ruin the rubber seal so it is impossible to ever use again.

We see castles and operas and villas. We befriend counts and wanderers and musicians and mafia men. We get drunk and drink coffee and sleep with strangers, but in the end, we fall in love with each other.

We hang our drawings on the walls and invite old philosophy professors over for wine. When the couch they are sitting on that we've made out of parts from the alley collapses beneath them, they keep right on talking like life falls out from under them all the time.

We pray in our own way and listen to so much music that every day has a soundtrack, every night a chorus. We are so alive and so present and so hungry that our bodies vibrate at all times, nonstop, for language, for sex, for food, for wine, for cigarettes, for adventure, for more of everything.

We write all the time and paint and cry and talk until we know every detail of even the lives we haven't lived.

She is my Italy Girlfriend, my Czechoslovakia Bride, my Little Mermaid, my Budapest Babe.

Of course, we break each other's hearts eventually.

Of course we do.

Wretched Excess

When I first arrive in Italy, I receive a letter from my Dad's Mom, Grandma Billie, telling me she's worried that I will be exposed to too much decadence abroad on my own. Yes! That is exactly what I want. I imagine soaking in every ounce of food and wine and men and beauty that a girl can. *Wretched excess* is my personal mantra. But instead of feeling fancy-free and bursting with life, drinking makes me homesick and lonely.

When Gwen leaves to spend spring break in Greece with her family, I am terrified of spending the week alone. Not because I fear for my safety, but because I fear unadulterated access to my thoughts and feelings. After saying goodbye to Gwen at the airport, I meet a man named Roberto on the night bus home. He says he's a music producer and pulls out a handful of CDs to show me. Would I like to go with him to the sea? He tells me he will buy me a return ticket that I can hold if I want to return. I say *yes* and we travel all night to the coast, drinking espresso when we arrive in the first hazy light of morning.

Roberto rents a room in an *albergo* and buys me a toothbrush. We spend the day on the beach drinking white wine and rubbing suntan lotion onto each other's backs. He is very tan and his face is old and starting to leather. He wears a speedo and I can see that he is very vain about his body. I tell myself that this is exciting, that I'm on an adventure, but in the end, I spend the night with this old man just so I don't have to be alone.

Frozen in Time

Gwen and I arrive in Copenhagen on Christmas Eve. Everything is closed so we eat the baguette in my backpack and find a hostel that will let us check-in. No one else is there so we have an enormous room full of empty bunk beds to ourselves and a bathroom that is essentially one large shower where we can stand under hot steam as long as we please. The hostel owner tells us of a free meal in Christiania for homeless people and travelers so we set out with his map scrawled on a napkin.

We expect the YMCA but we find a stone castle with an enormous banquet hall, torches, candlelight, and table after table piled with steaming heaps of meat and vats of potatoes and bottles of wine and it is pure magic—dancers and singers and pipes passed from hand to hand and the beautiful faces of strangers, a blur of light and color, young and beautiful, old and haggard. We dance and drink and sing and my Grandma Billie's parents were from Copenhagen so these are my people. I dance with a French boy who leans in close, his long black hair brushing against my face, and asks, *So is this what they mean by Sweet Virginia?*

We bring him back to the hostel with us and before dawn, the hostel owner bursts into our room screaming *GET OUT GET OUT,* his face tight and red with fury that we've brought a man into our bunk after our curfew, and without paying. We frantically stuff our clothes into our giant packs and burst out the door into the first light of morning where a vendor is selling hot dogs that we eat for breakfast at 5 am on Christmas Day, laughing now, and walking to see the Little Mermaid glisten in the water before we even sober up.

In Budapest on New Year's Eve we meet a short, dark man from the Hungarian mafia in the subway while we are making collect calls to our parents in the States as 1995 becomes 1996. In Budapest, we stay in a hostel that has a bar in its basement so we almost don't make it out alive. We go to the salt baths where we are naked and they scrub us down with bristle pads until our skin is raw and red and brand new.

In Prague, Gwen has a fever and I bring her oranges and peach juice and a man tries to kick in the door to our hostel. His boot carves a gaping hole as he screams *American Bitches!* and Gwen opens the door with my knife in her hand until he runs away. She is a Black Belt in karate so I feel safe with her and I'm falling in love with her and our lives are wound around each other like different strands in the same braid.

In Prague, we go see *Jesus Christ Superstar* in Czech and she memorizes the program notes and tells me she is Mary Magdalene. In Amsterdam, we smoke hash in the Red Light district and kiss men and then run away from them as fast as we can, because what we really want is to kiss each other but that won't happen until we're in Naples and that little town on the coast with all of the castles and the cats and then in Pompeii where we see the dead frozen forever in time, in space, in ash.

Your Body is Not a Thank You Note

My mother writes me a letter my senior year of college that says, *your body is not a thank you note*. In New York City at a fancy restaurant I try to take the bottle of wine the waiter brings to the table and Thomas laughs at my foolish mistake. I am so ashamed. Thomas borrows twenty dollars from me and when I ask for it back, he says I am far too emotional about money. His family owns a chateau in the south of France. I'm on scholarship and work at the movie theatre to pay my phone bill. I don't know how to act or what to say that doesn't expose me as poor and unsophisticated.

My body is not a thank you note, but there are so many men who can't read me at all.

White River Resort

After I graduate college in New York, I work as a cabin girl at the most remote dude ranch in Colorado. I want to get as far away from the snotty world of intellectual snobbery and elitist academics as I can.

When I get in the pickup truck with the two cowboys sent down to Denver to pick me up, I know I've chosen the right job for me. *Hey little lady, I want to bite your titty,* the older cowboy with the handlebar mustache says as I climb into the cab.

Shut up, Elmer, Big Will, the younger one, says. *We don't talk to ladies like that.* I laugh and pull out my flask and we drink whiskey and listen to Janis Joplin as we bounce up the jagged mountain road. I've never been pressed between two men in a truck cab before and I like it.

The White Eagle Resort is family-owned and the family is batshit crazy including the bosses' 13-year-old son Travis who bums Marlboro Reds off me and teaches me how to ride Hooker, the old mare who will die after suffering from moon blindness before the season is out.

I move into the girl's cabin with Kathy, who is part Native American and lives in the shadow of her twin, Karen. Karen rides horses hard and fast and has a real way with the cowboys.

My jobs at the ranch include lighting the fire in the woodstove in the lodge every morning at dawn, boiling the cowboy coffee, setting the tea in the sun to steep, setting the tables, taking meal orders from the staff and guests, washing the dishes with bleach in boiling hot water, scrubbing toilets, stripping beds in cabins, washing towels and bedding in the ancient wringer-washer, hanging sheets on the line to dry, running to tear the sheets down if it rains, cleaning out the oil lamps in the cabins, and mopping the shower room that everyone shares.

It is intense, exhausting work. The White River runs clear and fast through the valley, fireworks of wildflowers and coyotes and horses and wild birds everywhere.

Kathy gives me a Sioux dream catcher for protection and I spend the few hours I have off each afternoon writing and drawing and reading in the meadow. Ethyl, the 792-year-old pastry chef and matriarch of the family and I drink tumblers of wine from the boxes of red and pink we are given to sell to lodgers. But we never sell a single glass to anyone else. We drink it all ourselves.

We keep our beer in the creek and play poker at night. Sometimes we have liquor and bonfires and someone plays guitar and we slow dance to *Desperado* as if we are the last people living on earth. Big Will starts bringing me bouquets of wildflowers after his day-long rides up the mountain and I begin to accept them with growing anticipation.

Pussy Posse

The Pussy Posse is a group of women who like to ride both horses and cowboys hard and come up to the lodge for a week each summer. They have bleached blonde hair, tan leathery faces, and pink Wet n' Wild lipstick that glistens in the sun. They like their horses fast and their cowboys young. They order their toast dry, coffee black, and bacon well-done. I'm not worried about this so-called Pussy Posse until I see the look in Will's eye the morning after they arrive. *Oh no,* I say. *Oh no, you don't.*

I know Baby, he says. *I know. But they do expect me to take them on the far run.*

And that's all you'll do, I say. *Right?*

Right, he says putting his massive arms around me. *You don't have to worry your pretty little head about a thing.*

But the next day Matt comes to breakfast looking guilty and hungover as all hell and Janelle, the new cabin girl, won't speak to him through breakfast or lunch either. *Do it yourself,* she spits, throwing him a loaf of bread and a slice of ham when he slinks into the kitchen sheepish and hungry. *Get the Pussy Posse to make your fucking sandwich,* she says. I feel smug because Big Will has been with me all night turning away the older women's advances and surely losing a big ass tip because of it.

What did they have that I didn't? I would give him anything and he knew it. Not just sex either. He was in love with me. Anyone could see it.

You're done for, man, says Matt winking at Will. *Stick a fork in' him, ladies and gentlemen. He's done.*

Fuck off, says Janelle who says fuck so often it's more unusual if she doesn't. And that night she moves her stuff out of Matt's bunk into Elmer's, one bunk below and to the right.

One Condition

I am washing sheets in the wringer-washing machine when Big Will proposes down on one knee. My hair is in a messy ponytail and I'm half soaked from the jets of water shooting out of the hoses. *Valley, will you marry me?* he asks. *And if you say no today I'll ask you again tomorrow.*

Ok, then, no, I say and grin at him with big dumb love and a shiver of horror at the thought of getting married. The next day I'm washing dishes at the sink, my hands red from the steaming water and bleach, a blue apron soaked with suds. He slides his arms around my waist and says, *How about today? Will you say yes to me today?*

No, I say, but the idea has begun to ring with a certain appeal. How romantic and perfectly crazy to marry a wrangler. The next day I'm making the beds in a cabin, squeezing clean white sheets into too-tight metal bed frames.

Will you marry me? asks Will a third time. *Ok. Yes, I say. On one condition. That we don't tell anyone else about it.* Part of me knows this is all make-believe and saying it out loud will make it too real.

Great, says Will. *Awesome!* And that night he gives me his old wedding ring from his first marriage wrapped with tape so it won't fall off my finger. I'm engaged to a man who can ride horses and de-quill dogs attacked by porcupines and bench press entire trees but who can't remember how to spell my name. *Vally.*

In the Beginning

In the beginning, we only want to see her body. We know the bristle of her skin, the sheen of chestnut, the wiry barb of her coat, the untamed mane. My thighs know her broad back, her rippled muscles and rounded middle, her sensual, driving power, a bullet let loose from a gun, the sharp crack of her hooves, the orbs of her eyes that become lost to our solar system.

In the beginning, we just want to see her body become earth so it isn't lost to us completely, for good. We stuff cans of Budweiser in our apron pockets and pull on our boots. It will be a long walk to that far meadow if we can even find our way there— we just need to find her there. The sky is preparing for thunder, mixing up clouds and dust, heavy and pregnant with a darkening gray. We walk faster and faster as the drops begin to fall fatter and fatter and then faster and faster.

Janelle is shorter than me but quicker—a little ball of fire, we both take turns keeping up with each other. Past the river growing swollen with rain and past the field of wildflowers Big Will calls Sunflower Valley, farther than we've ever gone before on foot, alone without the cowboys.

And then we find her. Death is not a quiet or a simple thing. She is there and not there, negative space eating away at her insides, her magnificent body splayed and prone. To witness her death must have been like watching Goliath fall, a massive thing you can't imagine, so frail, so small, so in line with the wet mud of the earth. *She looks like shit,* Janelle says, observantly.

My belly stirs as I look at the rot and the wet and the stench and think of death. I know that the blood that hasn't come between my thighs for well over a month is more than chance, that my body is no longer, and never will, be mine alone again.

Hunting Season

It's getting colder and fewer families arrive, more hard-core Camo-wearing hunters eager to skin their deer on the grass and picnic tables surrounding the kitchen. They have lost all their shine and mystique for me. There's nothing romantic about their machismo now, just rednecks ready to kill helpless creatures at close range. Plus I am sick and exhausted, throwing up before I go to start the fire in the lodge each morning at dawn, unable to drink the cowboy coffee, retching as quietly and invisibly as possible while serving the eggs. I've avoided the actual words longer than I can avoid the deep knowing. The knowing that's growing in a sac of amniotic fluid in my belly while men curse and spit and kill all around me.

Kathy has stopped speaking to me, and it breaks my heart. I guess she's disgusted by the predictable, the newest cabin girl shacking up with a cowboy. Maybe my aura has gone dark and cloudy. I miss her and our talks and I wonder if the dream-catcher she gave me is still a blessing, or if it has become a curse.

For Hunting Season I've moved out of the girls' cabin into the bunkhouse with all the men and dogs. Big Will and I share an upper bunk, a truly impossible and even hilarious situation as he's 6'5" and I'm tender and sore and a single bed is really not enough for either of us alone, much less the two of us together. But all the other beds are taken by other wranglers and the dogs sleep on the floor.

After Will and I finally go to Denver to do what needs to be done I think I can finish out hunting season. Even if it is cold and dark and miserable it will be better than ending up back home with nothing, starting over from scratch.

Side Effects

One day I hear the phone ring by the back porch door, an unusual sound as the phone so rarely works at all. There are static pops but I hear my mother's voice coming through as if she's in the cabin beside me yelling out the door. *Valley!* she says. *Valley. Thank God. I've been trying to reach you, honey. Planned Parenthood called. They couldn't get through to you. Honey, they said the operation didn't take. You're still pregnant.*

My stomach sinks into my knees and my heart lands somewhere up near my throat.

Oh shit, I say. Oh *shit.* I had signed the form. *Possible side effects: nausea, cramping, pain, death, continued pregnancy.*

I remember feeling I'd prefer dying to the last item on that list.

Thankful

I don't remember packing. I don't remember who drives me away from the lodge or how I get to the airport but I do remember saying goodbye to the mountain, that feeling of leaving my heart in a place I'm not sure I'll ever see again. I remember crying on the plane and the kindness of the stranger beside me. A man or a woman, I don't know, but kindness with no questions asked and tissues given.

I'd had the second procedure at the same place that had botched the first. I just wanted it over and done. I hyperventilated, on the table. Stirrups will cause me to hyperventilate for years to come.

My mother meets me and my Percocet at the airport and carries us home. I spend days in bed moaning, a heating pad under my back, giant maxi pads between my legs, so much bleeding. She makes me tea and soup and tends me gingerly like I am still her baby. Thoughts of the lodge, of the river, of the mountains, soothe and haunt me.

Big Will calls on the phone when he can. I miss him and I hate him. When hunting season finally comes to an end, it's November. He asks if he can come see me and I say OK and he packs everything he owns onto a Greyhound Bus to Richmond. I pick him up on Thanksgiving at the bus station. He moves in with me that night and I try to feel thankful for something.

A Woman's Touch

Big Will and I live together at my mother's house for six months. He gets a job as a bouncer at a bar downtown and I get a job at a daycare on Lakeside. Big Will wants to quit drinking and go to AA but I tell him if he does, we're over. Drinking is the only thing making life bearable. When Big Will says we should move in with his Dad, I jump on the idea. It's either that or break up and I want to get the hell out of Richmond, and my mother's house.

We arrive in Arkansas with my new used Honda Prelude packed so tight we have to take out the spare tire. Big Will's Dad, Will Sr. is a widower. His third wife died after choking on a chicken bone at the diner up the street and he blames himself for not saving her. An aura of sadness hangs over the farm like a low slung cloud. I am sure a woman's touch will go a long way around here.

Will Sr.'s cabin only has a small living room, a kitchen and one bedroom so Big Will and I move into the tool shed. I don't mind at all, not even having to pee outside in the middle of the night or the sawdust and cobwebs because we are somewhere different, far from home.

The farm has two horses and a mule, chickens, a goose, cats, and a dog named Sally. There are rows and rows of vegetables and herbs, shiitake mushroom groves, and a large cash crop. In a good year, Will Sr. makes solid money on what he doesn't smoke himself. Even though I've come to loathe Big Will since the abortion, I am desperate to get out of Richmond. If not happiness, I feel like I might find something completely different than I've ever known before on this farm.

Morning Feather

On our 4th day on the farm, a filly is born. Big Will carries her in from the pasture in his hulking arms like she's a tiny baby. She is all legs and elbows sticking out everywhere. Will Sr. is proud of her as if she's his own child—he beams wide, love evident in his sad eyes. He asks me if I want to name her.

I do, but the only thing I'll ever really call her is Baby. My Baby. After all, this is around the time when my baby would have been born. We settle on naming her Morning Feather. She came to us at dawn and she's light as nothing. After a few hours Will Sr. says he's concerned. She's not nursing right, he says.

Lacy the Mare flares her nostrils and snorts and scuffs her feet in the dirt as the Wills try to balance the baby up on her feet. Lacy won't lay down and the baby's legs are too wobbly to stand. Will Sr. mixes her up some formula in the cabin while Big Will and I sit with her in the hay clucking and cooing like proud new parents.

Salty Dogs

Will Sr. lives in a dry county so we all pile in the cab of the pickup and drive across the county line to Ruby's liquor store. Ruby sells fresh eggs and special homemade pickles but we don't care about any of that. We pile the countertop with whiskey and beer and a couple of bottles of bad cheap wine. Back home, Will Sr. hands us big plastic tumblers of his specialty The Blackberry Cadillac: ice, ginger ale, and Manischewitz wine. We spend the next ten days trying to get Morning Feather to latch on while drinking as much as we can hold.

The men don't have jobs so I go out and get one at the five-star resort on the top of the mountain. I am a hotel maid and waitress, issued both cleaning supplies and a tuxedo I have to wash in the machine hooked up in the backyard. The black pants and white shirts on the line blow like ghosts in the wind. After every shift, I sit at the bar drinking salty dogs until it's time to drive back home to the boys who wait up for me so we can really get to drinking.

Next to his father, Big Will grows ever more diminished. Will Sr. is smooth and has a sharper wit and big, strong hands. Big Will and I no longer share anything more than a dead baby. As I grow to love the father, I grow to hate the son.

Blood Sacrifice

There's a goose that runs around giving orders to the chickens and taunting the mule. I can't remember his name though surely he has one, what would you name a wild goose? Why does Will Sr. suddenly decide it is time to slaughter and eat him? I don't know that either. He's never killed any of his chickens. We eat primarily straight out of the garden or cans from Walmart.

Maybe the farm demands a blood sacrifice or maybe Will Sr. needs to establish his role as the head of the family even though he doesn't work and I do. Maybe he feels the need to provide something we don't already have.

The goose does not go easily. The blade is not sharp and what should have been one smooth whack becomes a gory muscled sawing and hacking back and forth through feather and flesh and bone. The blood flows dark red and abundant into the soil and I try to force myself to watch because I want to be a part of everything that happens on the land but it makes my heart and stomach sick and soon I become aware that the blood is no longer just the goose's but Will Sr.'s too.

In the kitchen Will Sr. tells me to shake cayenne pepper into the bloody stump of his thumb as red swirls down the kitchen sink. Do we even eat the goose? Did we pluck him and cook him and serve him or do we bury him in a shallow grave? I don't remember because I became as cut off from my feelings that summer as the goose was from his head.

Visions

Melissa lives up on a hill in a house that seems like the skeleton of a whale that they'd stop building halfway through. She gives me *The Hobbit* and tips on how to get the most waitressing money at my job and how to get any man I set my sights on, too.

We meditate in her studio high on pot, surrounded by the furniture and gourds she paints and sells on the side of the road. She has dirty blonde hair and a hard tan face and eyes the color of the bluebells in the meadow. She has a family she's left behind, little girls who call and she talks to and who cry—but she has a new life and a new man and a new son now so she hangs up the phone and looks at me like *what are you gonna do?*

I miss my friends so I cling to Melissa when I can and in her way she looks out for me, tells me what she sees in her visions and how I can learn to have visions, too. One day she picks me up in her battered pickup to take me swimming in the quarry, just us girls. We undress behind a tree at the water's edge. Does she loan me a bathing suit or do we go naked?

The water is clear and freezing cold and I haven't been swimming in months. The tool shed doesn't have running water, much less a bathtub. I am grateful for the shock against my skin and the company of a woman in a wildland run by men. It isn't until we get out of the quarry and are pulling ourselves up to the dirt of the shore, yanking clothes over our cold wet skin that we see them, snakes swimming in circles around and through each other in endless loops and figure eights, their scaly gold bodies glittering in the sun. *Copperheads,* says Melissa and though we've escaped unharmed I still feel slick golden shivers ripple across my body all night long.

Cherry

Will Sr. and I make cherry jam from fresh cherries I pick right off the cherry trees. He gives me a pair of his wife's ruby red earrings and when I pack up her clothes for Goodwill, I try on her wedding dress and then keep a yellow raincoat and a pink negligee for myself.

We take rides on Lacy and the mule past fields and farms and forests, brambles scratching my bare arms as we race through the trees. At night I sleep in the barn, my body curled around Morning Feather, feeding her formula, begging her not to die.

Snakes and Worms

The day Morning Feather dies, I move out of the tool shed into the cabin. Big Will leaves early in the day on a Greyhound bus to visit his mother in California. Does he already know? Have I already told him? Are we still engaged?

Will Sr. and I bury the baby beneath the elderberry tree, the sky so lavender and pink you could cry. My first night in the king-sized bed is awful but I pretend it's good. I pretend I like being in his arms under his weight but I dream of snakes and worms writhing around in the earth until morning and I wake up screaming. *Shhh, it's Ok, Cowgirl,* Will Sr, says, *it's ok,* and he latches a leather bracelet around my wrist. It was his wife's before she died. He has white hair and a ruddy face and strong hands and a wide back. He's a few years older than my Dad.

Will Sr. takes me to a seafood restaurant for our first dinner out since I've come to the farm. We've only eaten from the garden and a shelf full of cans. I'm starved and the food is delicious but I can't really eat, it feels too much like stealing. After dinner, we drive through Dinosaur World, which is completely deserted, empty and strange.

The day I leave Arkansas, Will Sr. places the severed head of a buffalo on the picnic table in front of the cabin. He throws the massive dark hide over the fence and scrubs it raw with Borax on a Brillo pad. The glassy black eyes pull me and yank me in. I know in the glare that it's time to pack up and go, to leave this farm with the chickens and the mule and the horses and Sally the dog and the dead foal I've tried to save and my ex-fiancés father.

The eyes, horns, fur, and face have never left me alone, not for long. For years I felt as though I'd killed that buffalo, as though I'd severed his head from his body, had caused all his pain. That he wouldn't have been hurt if I hadn't left. Only recently did the healing come. When I met Buffalo in the Lower World on a shamanic journey, I knew I hadn't killed him, that instead he had been there protecting me, taking my pain to add to his own.

Lucky 13

I smoke a joint as I drive out of Arkansas and head west to meet Jenne and Edward in Denver. I play my mixtape of break-your-heart country songs about loving and leaving and driving and drinking in the player.

The wind picks up as I enter Kansas until I think perhaps Dorothy's tornado has come at last and my small car begins to sway to and fro on the highway. Around dusk, I stop at a Stuckeys for gas and a sandwich. The boy behind the counter is wearing a t-shirt that says *Lucky 13*.

Hear about them storms? he asks me.

I felt them, I say.

Looks like we're in for a big one, he says.

Well, shit, I say and when I tell him I'm sleeping in my car tonight, Lucky 13 sneaks me into a bedroom behind the Stuckey's in his family's home. Even though I'm finally safe, I go back out in the coming storm to find a 6-pack of beer, sleep in the Stuckey's with the door locked, and get back on the road before the sun rises in the morning.

Able to Fly

When I meet them in Denver, we're all wearing red tank tops. We stay at Jenne's parents' house in Lakewood and her parents, John and Sue couldn't be kinder or more gracious about feeding and housing a band of ragamuffin wanderers in their basement for days on end. But finally, it is time for Edward and me to go. We do acid while hiking the Rocky Mountains in Colorado which is terrifying and exhilarating.

In the Wind River Valley in Wyoming, high on XTC, we are visited by a tremendous and beautiful buck. We climb the Arches at the National Park in Utah and Edward encourages me to sing for him at night.

We cook rice and beans on Edward's camp stove and collect wild sage growing on the side of the road, burning it along with the weed we smoke in the tent and in the car and standing on cliff edges looking out over the expanse of the whole wild west.

When Edward and I arrive on the west coast we stay with my friend Matthew and his girlfriend at their house in Olympia. Our party becomes a week-long binge bordering on a long, extended blackout. Yoga at sunrise morphs into *Who's Afraid of Virginia Woolf?* by night. My wallet is stolen at a bar and though I didn't have much money left from Arkansas, now I have nothing at all.

Edward never complains about paying my way but I hate feeling broke and helpless and dependent, a feeling I am far too familiar with. He buys our plane tickets to Alaska and because I've kept my driver's license in my pocket, I am still able to fly.

The Last Frontier

In Juneau, we move into Edward's boyfriend's friend's trailer in a trailer park just outside of town. This move proves to be a crushing loss. Edward and his boyfriend are so thrilled to be together they do not need me. And Bronwyn, the owner of the trailer, does not want me in her trailer at all. I am penniless and completely dependent on others to take care of me. And though Edward is happy enough to pay my way, Bronwyn is cold as the ice around us so I spend as much time as I can in the woods beyond her small yard. And this is where I turn 23, broke, friendless, and alone.

When I can't stand it anymore, I set out on my own to find a job. I walk into Juneau along the side of the highway, hugging the guardrail, wearing my best skirt with my hair in a bun. I pray for God to help me find a job and at Glacier Bay Tours and Cruises, the very first building I enter in town, I do. *Are you hiring?* I ask the pretty lady behind the desk. *You'll want to talk to Gino,* she says and sends me upstairs to meet the Captain of the Fleet.

Women Like You

Gino is short but handsome with high cheekbones and dark, black eyes. He is half Inuit and half Italian I discover during our interview which feels like a first date. I am desperate and he is handsome and he has what I need.

I love women like you, he tells me. *So brave and so fearless traveling alone, far from home.*

I can't believe he called me a *woman*. It's true that I'm brave but I'm also hungry and want to stop eating off someone else's dollar.

Oh, I love traveling, I tell him. *I feel like Gulliver,* I say.

I have an early edition of Gulliver's Travels, he says. *I'll give it to you,* but he never does. Instead, he tells me about his band and his acting gigs and how his birthday is on the vernal equinox when the world is equal parts day and night.

So, am I hired? I ask.

Can you leave this week? he asks.

I can, I say.

Perfect, he says. *You'll just need to take a Coast Guard-issued drug test before you go.* He says this sentence carefully, studying my face. My eyes grow big and my brow grows tight and he pulls me over towards him and points me towards the window where we look out at the rooftops of the buildings, shops, and bungalows on the sloping hill of the city.

If a certain person, he says, *were to go to a certain health food store and buy a certain tea, that person would pass the drug test,* he tells me, his fingers tracing a map on the glass. *But you didn't hear that from me,* he says.

Hear what? I say, my heart pounding both because I need to go find that tea and because he is very handsome and before the interview is over, he says he thinks he is falling in love with me.

I leave his office and walk straight through town to the health food store at the intersection of Gino's fingers. The cashier doesn't bat an eye, this must be an everyday purchase around here. Back at the trailer, I drink so much I think I might drown. When I take the test I am horrified to discover the results will take two weeks to come back. If I fail they will remove me from the boat while I am out at sea.

Wilderness Discoverer

The day I set sail aboard the Wilderness Discoverer, Edward and his boyfriend come to wave goodbye to me, but it is Gino I look for as the dock grows smaller in the distance. I don't know when I'll see him again. I've found black pants and black shoes at a thrift store but I'm given a company-issued starched white button-up, a black fleece vest, and a heavy winter coat with the fleet's emblem emblazoned over each breast.

As I'm joining the boat midseason everyone already knows each other, and I'm assigned an empty top bunk in the girls' quarters in the bowels of the ship. The purser, Renee, takes me under her wing and introduces me to the crew. Captain Jamie, Scott the Chief Engineer, Mark the First Mate and most importantly my immediate superior, Patrick the Chief Steward. Patrick is slight and tall and handsome and I know we'll get along.

I'm not so sure about the other stewardesses and deckhands though. Many are already burned out, sleep-deprived, and ready to jump ship at a moment's notice, which during the course of the season sailing on our 5-day loop through Alaska's Eastern Passage, many of them do. April, a tall blonde deckhand approaches me on the Lazdek as I'm staring dreamily out to sea.

Do you love him too? she asks and she doesn't need to say who.

Sea Foam

My jobs include vacuuming the endless, long, narrow halls and the dining area after each meal. Crab night is always the worst, flecks of shell and flesh embedded in every square inch of stubby carpet. I scrub heads, make beds, set the big banquet tables, sort silverware hot out of the industrial cleaner and fold cloth napkins into origami swans, roses, bowties, and crescent moons. Patrick repeats the origami patterns for me again and again, until my hands hold the muscle memory of the folds.

The work is mindless and repetitive but made bearable by talking with Patrick who is 38 and dating another stewardess, Autumn who is only 18. At 23, I feel wise—and old.

Occasionally Patrick promises to do chores for me if I write poetry for him. I write haiku after haiku about seafoam and true to his word, he does the vacuuming. He also gives all of us stewardesses roses with poems by a Chinese poet about girls lost at sea that I find beautiful and sad. But it isn't Patrick I feel the jolt of current with—it's Marc who is tall, strong, broad-shouldered, handsome, and deaf.

Marc and I take our breaks in Sitka running to the market to buy
strawberries and whipped cream, eating them and kissing in the tall
grass while he teaches me ASL and we talk about the ocean with
our hands.

I have left it all
Home, land, lovers, friends foes, time
For mist and seafoam

Sky threw a party
God wore his top hat and
Seafoam kissed his brow

No letters today
I trace my name in seafoam
So the fish will write

Since you threw the last
Flask of champagne in the sea
I'm drunk on seafoam

Little boy trapped in
The belly of an orca
Has no strings attached

Dry as a Bone

Whales are everywhere. From the ship I see grays, humpbacks, and orcas breaching and slapping tails, flipping and flopping and doing their wild dances upon the water. There are eagles and puffins and in the rivers, black bears stand tall in the fast-flowing water opaque with salmon, swiping up their dinner with powerful paws.

Marc is transferred from our ship to another in the fleet where he can work in the galley instead of on deck, a job too dangerous without perfect hearing. I am sad when he leaves but not broken. He signs *I'll see you around,* and I sign *my friend, goodbye.*

I see Gino briefly between cruises and occasionally he gives me something but never stays to talk with me long. A book of poetry, his CD, a picture of himself with long dark hair looking like an Inuit Johnny Depp. I put my hand to my heart and daydream about him as I stare out at the churning sea.

After a few weeks, I begin to worry less about my drug test coming back positive and more about how I am going to survive the rest of the season without any alcohol, dry as a bone. When feelings surface it's like nails and needles and icicles piercing me in the gut and the womb. I long to numb, to go under, to anesthetize the feelings I don't know how to handle on my own.

Staff and crew are responsible for passenger safety at all times and drinking is strictly forbidden. I have not had to face a night sober for so long I've forgotten what it feels like. I miss red wine with a steady undercurrent of longing as for a lover, or a father who was never really home.

One day in Skagway when no one else is around, I sneak into a bar and order Kahlua and coffee, desperate for a moment's reprieve from my restless mind. A chalkboard on the wall of the dark bar says *Every plant has to grow through a lot of dirt to bloom.* I am devastated that after a second round, I still feel nothing at all.

Dry Land

My knuckles are busted from cramming sheets into bed frames. I'm tired of smelling like Clorox and industrial cleaner. We aren't given more than a few hours off at a time, even over a period of months, and it's quite common for crew to never come back from a break in Skagway or Sitka or Glacier Bay. Even with the whales and the moose and the eagles and the bears, we are surrounded by mountains of ice, glaciers of frozen cold. And this is a place where people have already—or are about to—lose it all.

I miss having an entire day to myself, sleeping in a real bed, and drinking. I miss drinking like life itself. My insides feel hollow again and I'm dying for something to fill them up. I call my Mom collect from a payphone on a dock over the Lynn Canal. She accepts the charges and listens quietly as I tell her I don't think I can take it anymore. I need a break. I might even come home.

Valley, she says finally. *Big Will called. He found out about you and his Dad. He said he has a gun. He wants to kill you or himself. Valley, stay on the boat. Don't step foot on dry land.*

Fuck, I say, *Fuck.* What does my Mom say? She doesn't shame me or make me feel bad. *Stay safe,* she says. *Take care of yourself. Call me again soon,* she says. *I love you.*

The Birthday Streamers
of the Gods

Patrick bangs on my cabin door at 2 AM. We have so few passen-
gers we've each been given a cabin of our own. The cabins are tiny
but feel like a palace after the top bunk in the bowels of the ship
scraping over icebergs. I drag myself out of bed as Patrick continues
down the hall banging on door after door.

We stream out of our rooms bleary and disheveled and make it to
the bow of the ship, magnets drawn to the eerie green and yellow
breaking sky. The Northern Lights are like the birthday streamers
of the Gods and soon we're awake for real, wide-eyed spreading out
on benches to watch the show.

I lie down next to Avo and we stay up talking long after everyone else
has gone back to bed. Avo is short for Avocado but his real name is
Bob and we tell each other our life stories dramatized under Alaskan
skies. Avo says he can astral travel and when we finally go to bed to
sleep, he says he'll visit me in my dreams. But it's not Avo I see in the
galley when I wake up the next morning. It's Gino—I've never seen
him outside of Juneau, much less while our ship is at sea.

Gino gathers the crew together and in a hushed tone tells us he'll be with us for the next few days. Captain Jamie has been evacuated from the ship under allegations of sexual harassment from Renee the Purser and we are under quarantine for the remainder of the investigation.

Can we have tea later? Gino asks me in the hall after his debriefing.

I'd love to, I say, and go to change out of my starchy uniform into a skirt. All of us stewardesses are always longing to wear our real clothes, to stretch out past black pants and collared white shirts, to transform from the maids we are into the mermaids we wish we could be.

Powerful Women

Gino knocks gently on my door. *Come in,* I say. *The lock's broken.*

I can fix that for you, he says before sitting next to me on the bed.
We haven't been alone together since our interview the day he
hired me and my palms feel hot and sweaty. *So. Captain Jamie and
Renee,* I say.

Yes, he says. *She left on a skiff in the middle of the night. Jamie says they
just had a flirtatious banter. That nothing actually happened. We'll get
to the bottom of it,* he says, and I feel his thigh move imperceptibly
closer to mine. *It's all so crazy,* I say and I don't know if I'm talking
about Jamie or Gino and the months at sea I've dreamed of a
moment just like this one. *I know,* he says. And then he says, *Valley,
beautiful women have the power to create or destroy. Be careful which
one you choose.*

What do you mean? I ask. I feel like he's the one with the power. He
takes my face in his hand and turns it so we are looking into each
other's eyes.

It would be very dangerous for me to kiss you right now, he says and grabs his hand back as if it's been stung. *But that's the whole point, right? The danger?* Then he pats me on the knee, pulls a knife out of his pocket and jiggles it into the door until I hear the latch click. *It's fixed now, he says halfway in the door, halfway out. Be sure to keep it locked. And,* he says, backing slowly away, *Here's my card. Give me a call if you need an oil change in Seattle.*

The Real Journeys

After four months of this cycle at sea, when the boat docks at last, I count down the minutes, not just until I'm free of the boat, but until I'm allowed to drink again. A few deckhands and I run to the closest bar we can find. I order a glass of cheap red wine and slam it back like a shot. Nothing happens. I begin to feel small hammers clang in my head and I want to shut my eyes. But there is no ecstatic escape or topsy turvy oblivion. There is only dull pain and the desire for sleep. Something is wrong with that glass of wine so I order another one. Same thing but worse. It must be a bad bar.

We go to another bar. Here I order whiskey and sling it back. But no matter how many bars I go to or how many different drinks I order, I am not able to get drunk that night, and in fact, I am never able to get drunk again.

I call my mother collect from a payphone where the ship is docked. *Valley*, she says, *Uncle Tom's getting married. I think you should come home.*

But I'm not done traveling, Mom, I say. I have a vague sense of going next to Sedona, and Yellowstone, and the Grand Canyon.

The real journeys aren't out there, she says. *They're inside you. Besides, it's Rosh Hashanah.*

Ok, I say. *But just for a little while,* and I buy a train ticket cross country back to Richmond, home.

The Book of Life

That first night off the boat is like climbing into bed after hours in the ocean. The sheets sway to and fro. I don't know if I can sleep on dry land. I leave the motel the next morning with my army bag of clothes and a Gideon's Bible stolen from the bedside table.

On the train, I sit next to a tall muscled blonde boy and when I sleep, my head rests on his shoulder. We share bagels from my bag and drink beers in the lounge car. When *Wings of Desire* comes on the train TV, I think *I'm meant to be a messenger of light. God wants me to be a messenger of light.* I don't know where this thought comes from because I feel like my entire body is a secret wrapped in a lie. I'm terrified that once I'm home everyone will see right through me.

The boy and I make out in the tiny compact bathroom, and I say goodbye to him in Chicago. It's always easy to find love on trains. I open Gideon's Bible from my bag and read Psalm 139.

> *Oh Lord, you have searched and known me. Where shall I flee from your spirit?... If I ascend to heaven God, you are there, if*

I take the wings of the morning and dwell in the uttermost parts of the sea, even there your hand shall lead me.

In a fitful sleep, I dream my mother serves me boiled purple underwear for my welcome home dinner. The little boy in front of me says to his mom, *Jonah was in the belly of the whale? That's just like Pinocchio.* And it's just like me. I've been spit from the belly of the whale onto the shores of home. It will soon be Yom Kippur. What do I have to do to be inscribed into the Book of Life for another year?

At the train station, my mother tells me the good news. The man renting our old house across the street from her new house has just moved out so I have a place to stay. The tiny house I'd grown up in feels like a playboy mansion after the bunk on the ship and now I have my own kitchen, too.

Free Therapy

A letter arrives from Big Will and I shudder as I hold its solid weight in my hand. I read it once, fast, and never again. Twenty pages of accusations and hate, all of it well deserved. This is the stuff of Greek tragedy my mother says, though I think it's more like Jerry Springer.

Big Will calls me a *fat cunt* and says if I don't send him everything he's ever given me he will come to get it himself. Even a glance at the velvet and blue jean dress he bought me in Denver makes me feel sick. I pack everything into the trunk and mail it out west by freight, but I still don't feel better.

Mom, I think I need to go to therapy, I say.

I know some therapy that's free, she says. *There's a women's AA meeting at the church up the street.*

But do you have to think you're an alcoholic? I ask.

You can wonder, she says. And so I go to my first AA meeting but decide I'll have to give back the white chip l pick up because I'm not an alcoholic. I know this because I can't get drunk anymore, no matter how hard I try.

I learn that my stepbrother's girlfriend left her car in Richmond and I left mine where she lived in Seattle so we decide to trade. A week home from Alaska, I have a home I will live in for nearly the next 19 years, a car, a white chip, and an ex-boyfriend who wants me dead.

Black and White

Black-and-white thinking is the topic at my first AA meeting. I relate to every word, existing only in the extremes. My friend Bryan says that when he turns 40 in August he plans to be done with the binary thought system. *It's too Manichean,* he tells me. I have to look up *Manichean.* A religious system of thought based around good/evil, all/nothing, light/dark. Is there really any other way though, I wonder?

Writing helps me integrate. So do prayer and meditation and the prolonged experience of living. But I wonder if some part of me won't always be Jekyll and Hyde, good and bad, above and below. I relate to Persephone and her relationship with Hades. I relate to women who snap, who go insane and forsake all the good they have. That part of me will always exist, no matter how good, how beautiful my life, I hear the siren call of self-destruction. I'm trying to live, to make my peace with the world in-between.

Cutting Off Your Arm

Would you rather cut your arm off all at once or piece by piece? my mother asks.

Thirty days sober, I decide to quit smoking.

I throw out my cigarettes and she takes me to get a manicure. I beat my couch with a Wiffle ball bat, full of frozen rage and grief, melting fast. The house I grew up in is my detox unit, my halfway house.

When I open a bank account with the money I've made on the cruise ship in Alaska, the teller says, *I honor your spirit.* I use $300 to buy a used refrigerator and food and enough time until I can hold a job. My belongings are stuffed in an army duffle bag and attics everywhere. I have a few clothes and a polyester patchwork quilt I bought on the side of the road in Arkansas that I've used as a blanket, a dress, a tent, a flag.

I go to meetings in every part of the city. This is how I travel now.

I hide all of my old music from myself—my wild, sad, beautiful, heart-wrenching whiskey and drugs and wine and smoke music. I listen to classical music I've never heard instead. I write in my journal about my misery and my bad luck and wait like hell for what my mother promises will be the most beautiful spring of my life.

Bread Crumbs

I meet him when I am just a few days sober. At 6'5", a football player and wrestler, I write him off as a big dumb jock. My theory, however, is upended when he leaves *The Razor's Edge* by Somerset Maugham on my doorstep, with a short critical analysis comparing the main characters to the two of us in the book jacket. *The Razor's Edge* is followed by *The Pilgrim*, a treatise on the value of praying without ceasing, and then a war novel by Steinbeck. The coup de grace is a journal full of letters he's written, addressed directly to me. His words are bread crumbs I follow, leading me straight to his door.

His face invades my dreams. The blonde hair and blue eyes of a Ken Doll morph into the golden features of a Sun God. He is, I learn, wealthy, powerful, and determined to break me. I've resolved not to date anyone during my first year of sobriety but it is his mission to change my mind. I almost fold, he almost wins. But I make it to a year before I say yes. By now I've been warned about him. *A predator*, they say. *Watch out*, they say. *I can't*, I say. It's too late for me. I am sunk.

On our first date, the car phone rings and he answers it. *It's me,* I hear a woman's voice breathe through the line. *I have to go,* he says to her and hangs up, but *it's me* rings in my ears the whole night. The energy between us is so intense I can't hear what he is actually saying. He stares at the waitress long after she leaves our table.

We go to a dance together on New Year's Eve, ringing in the new century side by side. I dream that he picks me up with his ex-wife and small children in the back seat of the car. Still, I let him have me. It's like rolling down an icy slope. There is no slowing the trajectory in motion. After making his kill he is sated and he stops calling at all.

I mourn like the sun has dropped from the sky.

Book 2:

A House with Hundreds of Rooms

I had another dream about lions at the door
They weren't half as frightening as they were before
But I'm thinking about eternity
Some kind of ecstasy got a hold on me

— Bruce Cockburn, *Wondering Where the Lions Are*

Past Life Regression

Joan leads me to her bedroom upstairs. I have driven to her house in Mechanicsville following directions scribbled down in my journal. She greets me at the door with a cigarette and a miniature poodle under one arm.

Girl! she says, staring me down. *You got a man coming into your life! Come with me.* I follow her up the carpeted stairs. I am here for a past life regression because I desperately need to find, and then fix, what's wrong with me. *Get undressed,* she says, and I strip down to bra and underwear and step into her sweat lodge, a tall, narrow wooden box that plugs into her wall. It's hot and dry and I suck in my breath and close my eyes and feel quills of heat prick my skin.

Joan beats a drum and chants, and I pray I'll sweat out all the poison that's consumed me.

When I'm out of the box she wraps me in a towel and leads me to a massage table in the center of the room. Lying on my back, I close my eyes as she counts down from 20, leading me down a long flight of stairs. When she tells me to look down I see leather sandal straps crisscrossed over my feet. Heavy cloth from white linen floats around my ankles. *I am in a temple,* I tell Joan. *I am a priestess. A golden-skinned man with sun-colored hair approaches me. He towers over me. I cower under him. He is beautiful. He is a god. He is a killer. He is going to kill me.*

Men hurt you, Joan says. *You are scared of men. It's time you reclaim your power!* She waves her hands over my chest in great figure eights in the air above me, sweeping away death, betrayal, and fear. She prays and chants and asks my guides and angels to heal me, to bless me, to make me whole. Tears stream down my face. I hug her and thank her and drive home, exhausted.

That is Friday afternoon. On Saturday afternoon, a guy from my meetings leaves a message on my answering machine. *I haven't seen you in a month of Sundays,* he says. *Would you like to get dinner?* I call him back to say *yes.* I wear a sundress with spaghetti straps and we go to the Grape Leaf, a Greek restaurant at a strip mall near my house. We may as well be in Greece. I feel safe and beautiful and at ease sitting across from Stan at dinner as we share a plate of olives and feta and grape leaves and spanakopita.

This is our first date. It is June 2, 2000.

We get married one year later to the day.

When We Meet

I'm wearing thick-rimmed black glasses and a jean jacket vest covered in my mother's buttons. He's wearing a flannel shirt with penny loafers. The first time we see each other at an AA meeting neither one of us can tell what the hell the other one is about. He always has a yo-yo and when I quit smoking he gives me one, too. *So you'll have something to do with your hands,* he says.

I dream that we sail around the world on a small ship and then that we run a marathon and collapse together into the dirt, exhausted after crossing the finish line. So I don't have to lay my head on the ground, he puts his hand under my head to use as a pillow. The tenderness of this gesture, even though it's only a dream, breaks my heart.

He calls to ask me for information about my Dad's trip to build houses in Honduras after Hurricane Mitch, then hangs up as soon as I've told him. I burst into tears when I put down the phone. He refuses to have anything to do with me outside of large groups for over a year because old-timers are supposed to leave newcomers alone to get sober.

Instead of asking me out, he goes to Honduras and builds houses for people left devastated by the storm.

Water Seeks Its Own Level

The first trip we take together is to the Shenandoah Valley. We pass through a town called Stanley, and I take photographs of my new tall, dark and handsome boyfriend in front of the Stanley Post Office. His grandfather, uncle, and nephew are all named Stan, too. I have entered a brand new world.

I buy yellow silk lingerie which he peels off as soon as we lock ourselves in our cabin at Skyland resort, a few miles from where my Dad grew up and where my aunts worked their first jobs. In the morning we eat blueberry pancakes and drink dark rich coffee and take a trail ride on horses.

When we hike the trails through the mountains, he picks up every piece of litter he sees on the ground while butterflies circle his head like a halo. Back home he doesn't even look at my friends and I have no qualms going to the bathroom or leaving him in a room with other women.

Friends ask us if we'll take care of a dog for the weekend—a rescue, a pit bull puppy who has been abused. We adopt her immediately and name her Hermione after the character in the first Harry Potter novel that has just come out. He loves her fast and hard which makes me love him, too. My cat sits in his lap. The puppy plays with his boots and his hands. He carries Hermione around in his arms like a baby. The cat and I are impressed. Soon the puppy and the cat and the man join me for almost every meal. I bring Hermione to his apartment and she sleeps between us in his bed, her blonde fur our blanket. I tell him I'm afraid; I tell him I want everything. *Water seeks its own level*, he says and we fall asleep, hands clasped around each other, and our dog.

Fixer Upper

As kind as he is, there's a certain brooding darkness about Stan that catches my eye and worries me, too. *He could be a project,* I tell my friend Selvy, an art therapist. I can tell by looking at him that he can fix anything, but I sense there's something still broken inside of him, too.

I've been sober a few months and Selvy's been sober nine years, occasionally smokes my cigarettes, and brings me Chinese food cooked by her Indian mother. ***He's** a fixer-upper?* she laughs. *Honey, what about **you?***

I am a year sober, a year off the ship, unemployed, driving a piece of shit car, crying my eyes out every day, and still crazy from coming off drugs and alcohol and weird affairs with strange men.

Maybe she's right. Maybe I'm a piece of work, too.

A House with Hundreds of Rooms

The first time I follow Stan to his house he drives like a grandma so I don't lose him. At a red light, he jumps out of his car, runs up to my open driver's side window, kisses me, and then jumps back into his car in time for the green. The first time we kiss he tells me he feels like he's going to have a heart attack. Every kiss after feels like a reverberation of that moment, the electric meeting of lips deep beneath a quiet black ocean.

On Valentine's Day, he gets a star in the Cigna swan constellation named after me on a framed certificate with the coordinates. It is the best gift I've ever received. I buy him stamps and sealing wax with his initials, a pocket watch with a long silver chain he ties to his belt loop.

Our schedules flow together like concurrent rivers and we have dinner together every night and then increasingly breakfast together in the morning. None of our friends are surprised. *Called it!* they say. *We knew long before you two,* they say. *We knew.*

I have never felt this way about anyone before. My heart has always been a house with hundreds of rooms, each waiting to be filled with something different or someone new.

The Very First Time

I say *I love you* the very first time we have sex, right in the middle. I say it because I can't not say it. I say it because it's true. I say it first. I've waited two long weeks, 14 interminable days, an eternity of waiting to be intimate. He's gone to visit his sister and her newborn baby and when he calls to tell me about them, as he described the baby's toes, I think, yes. I decide right then, *yes. I am ready.*

He looks like the statue of David I saw in Italy. All of that marbled muscle, the triangle of broad shoulders angling towards narrow hips. I can feel in his eyes and in his hands, in his mouth on my neck, around my cradled breasts, from the rolls of my thighs to the forest of my calves, as he runs his tongue along the arch of my foot that the current of this electricity runs both ways. He holds me like his hands are made of steel, looks at me like I am a feast. Still, I catch his hand when he reaches to turn on the light. That first is the one that will take more time.

We fly kites together in my Dad's field the next day, wind whipping our hair into a storm and he tells me that he loves me, too.

Inheritance

The day Stan moves into my childhood home he crashes his car into another car at the intersection of Broad and Meadow. He doesn't stop at the red light because he isn't looking at the red light. He is looking at me. We are looking at each other's faces, stupid with love. We have no clue what's coming next. No one is hurt but we step out of our cars and wait until the police come and then exchange insurance policies. That night, Stan moves in.

My mother's button business is still in the back bedroom of the house we rent from her. Stan piles his tools and motorcycles and lawn equipment in the shed on top of everything my father and stepfather and other previous tenants have left behind. It looks like a boat that can't hold any more water sinking to the bottom of the sea.

The house is far from perfect but it's in a quiet neighborhood unlike Stan's apartment in Oregon Hill where the roof is falling in and his next-door neighbor was recently robbed and stabbed.

My mother sells us this house a year after we get married. She says it's cheap because it's our inheritance. Stan replaces my tube TV that only gets three channels with a sleek new flat screen and sets out to fix the broken, the leaky, the unhinged everywhere else.

As soon as he fixes one thing another thing breaks and it's impossible to stay on top of everything the house demands.

Strange New Land

We go to Chincoteague for our honeymoon, where my Dad had
honeymoons with each of my two stepmothers. We stay in
Plum Cottage, all yellow with purple trim and a tiny kitchen, a tiny
bathroom, and a tiny bedroom, which at first I think is all I
need in this world, or at least for this honeymoon.

We go hiking and kayaking and fly kites on the beach. But something
is missing from this island paradise. I don't know what it is until I
meet Michelle, a wild-eyed long-haired psychic artisan who spends
her days weaving baskets. I beg her to teach me. *Meet me tomorrow
at noon,* she says.

You're doing *what?* my new husband asks. I'm trying to prove I can
still do something on my own, even if I'm someone's wife. I labor
and sweat and curse over the brittle reeds of my basket until they are
bent into something beautiful.

On our last day on Chincoteague, we walk into a white clapboard Methodist Church on the side of the highway and ask the seven-foot-tall Jamaican minister to give us a blessing. We kneel at his feet beside the cross, holding hands together in this strange new land and we pray.

Scrapbooking

When we get back from Chincoteague, I begin to scrapbook. I don't want to forget anything. I need to make sense of everything. Lots of ladies in AA are scrapbooking, and specialty stores are cropping up all over town. Only they don't have the stickers I need to make my photo collages realistic—spilled wine, joints, crumpled packs of cigarettes. I do what I can with sparkly alphabet letters and pom-poms. I cut my photos into shapes and glue them into tiny paper frames. This way they seem a little more contained.

I become a scrapbook distributor and go to classes and conventions and set up scrapbooking parties with my friends but after all of the supplies I buy for myself, I don't make any money.

So I take up crocheting and then sewing and then I make a bunch of stained glass magic wands. All to avoid the one thing that terrifies me most: writing it all down.

Too Good to Be True

Three weeks after our wedding, Stan and I go to La Diff, an upscale furniture store with a $50 gift card we've received. Fifty dollars isn't enough to buy a doorstop at La Diff, but we have fun looking at the fancy furniture and dreaming. I imagine one day off in the distant future actually buying a brand new couch and having a house big enough that it will fit in.

While I'm fantasizing about stuffed armchairs and end tables, I notice that Stan is no longer at my side. I wander around looking for him and when I don't see him, I check the second floor, and then the third. He's not anywhere. Finally, I take the elevator all the way down to the parking garage to see if our car is still there. We have been married three weeks and my husband has left me. I knew it was too good to be true. I knew I would never be able to keep a man. But the car is still in the parking spot where we left it. A moment later, Stan is stepping out of the elevator looking relieved. *I couldn't find you anywhere!* he says. *Where did you go?*

Where did you go? I ask and fall into his chest, weeping.

Married Woman

We've been married for six months when my face blows up like a hot air balloon. My cheeks are ruddy and round, my thighs, arms, and belly inflated. I feel like the Pillsbury Doughboy.

Honey, you can't just eat everything you see, the nurse says after she weighs me. I have gained 50 pounds since my wedding day. The buffalo hump arrives next, above my shoulders, below my neck, like I am wearing shoulder pads, like I'm an 80s female exec, a football player, Quasimodo.

I am a married woman now and maybe this is what married women look like. When I feel a pop in my right side, I go back to the doctor, and this time they give me an ultrasound. They can't explain the pop, but they do find a tumor on my adrenal gland pumping out cortisol. *Cushing's disease.*

I rush surgery, beg them to cut me open, carve the tumor out. Is it malignant? We don't know but Stan and I watch movies about women dying from cancer and weep while we wait to find out.

Maybe Stan's married the last of me like Jenny and Oliver in *Love Story*. Maybe I signed away who I was on a document filed at City Hall in exchange for this new buffalo version of myself.

Surgery is six hours long, my scar a jagged lightning stripe stapled together around my middle. When I wake up, the doctor tells me that in addition to the tumor and adrenal gland, he's taken out a rib.

I am the reversal of Eve. I am the bride of Frankenstein. What of me is left?

Alien

At a beachfront condo in North Carolina, I sob to my husband. *I'm not skinny and tall and blonde and perfect like your family!*

I didn't marry them, he says. *I married* **you.**

A short emotional Jewish girl with a fat ass, I say.

Yes, he says. *I love you,* he says and kisses my tears.

His tall, blonde, skinny family couldn't be more loving, warm, or accepting but nonetheless, I feel like an alien that has landed in their midst.

First Pregnancy

In my wedding vows, I say that I want to have lots of babies. Stan has told me that he wants us to have at least nine so we can form our own baseball team. I've been told more than once that I have child-bearing hips.

I have always imagined myself as a mother. When the pregnancy test is positive, I am ecstatic. We both are. I've seen Stan hold babies and play with puppies. He is a natural dad. Everything is happening right on time, according to schedule, even though it's a schedule I never imagined I'd follow. Graduate from college, fall in love, get married, buy a house, have a baby. This isn't happening to the friends I expected it to and yet to my surprise, it's happening to me.

We Save Nothing

It is a difficult nineteen weeks with many days of bleeding and bed rest. At my doctor's visit, the nurse is unable to find a heartbeat with her fetal monitor.

This happens sometimes, she says, but she is paging the doctor. The doctor can't find a heartbeat either. They let me stay in the room as long as I need, to gather myself. Office hours are over and they are packing up, ready to go. It is like my real life has stopped here, and the story of my life is about to begin. There are terrible decisions to be made. Do we hold a service or plant a tree? Do I allow them to take her remains or do I request to keep them, to see and to bury?

In the end, they put me out and we save nothing.

I bite my tongue under anesthesia. It is swollen and sore. The recovery room nurse takes a look at it. *It's not that bad,* she says.

Thuck you, I say.

I despise pregnant women. I avoid them like lepers. I cross to the other side of the street, dart to the next aisle at the grocery. I give their fat bellies the evil eye, curse their able hips, turn my back on what looks to be easy, effortless bliss.

We fight over what to keep and what to give away. I want to put it all in the attic. I want to know it is there, safe, untouched, even if I never look at any of it again. But he wants to give it away, be rid of it, not have it hanging, literally, over our heads.

One night at dinner, Stan offers a stroller to his co-worker whose wife is expecting their third child. *How dare you?* I seethe. I glare at them, push away from the table, refuse to return.

Friends bring roasts and cooked carrots and pound cakes. They sit on the edge of the bed, stop in unexpectedly, send cards, call throughout the day. It is not enough. It is all wrong. The words they say bend and fold and are packed away before I can open the door to watch them leave.

God's Child

When it happens again, the doctor lets me leave through the back door without paying. I am weeping, hysterical, hiccupping. A huge man is in the hall with his two small boys. He stops the elevator door with his shoulder and takes my hands in his massive fist.

He bows his head in prayer. *Dear Jesus,* he says. And then *Jesus something something Jesus. May the blood of Jesus wash over you,* he prays for me. I have a vision of Jesus standing over me, his blood dripping down my head. I start to laugh. He can't tell. He thinks I'm still crying. He lets the elevator door go and I begin the descent. Thank you, Jesus.

An obese Jewish man from AA tells me that my ancestors suffered so that I could have a better life. They were slaves in Egypt, settled in Israel, endured the Holocaust. *Your problems are small,* he says. *Your worst fears haven't even happened.* Fuck you, fuck you, fuck you.

The phone rings; I don't answer it. The phone rings; I don't answer it. The phone rings; I don't answer it. Take a message. She's not here.

She's busy. She's preoccupied. She can't come to the phone. Do you want to leave a message?

I haven't met any other writers in here, says Blessy, my IV nurse. I guess other writers' babies don't die, and if they do, they don't go to Henrico Doctor's Hospital to have them removed.
This is all part of God's plan I think. No, it isn't. Yes, it is.

I ask God why he didn't give me these babies. God says, *I did.*

Just Do Something

I am sitting at my desk when the bleeding begins. I now have a new job at Seven Hills, a progressive middle school for boys. The headmaster and his assistant are talking behind closed doors and I am in charge of the hallway.

I really should alert someone, shut down the computer, tidy my desk and return 6 or 7 phone calls, but the sobs blooming in my chest force me down the stairs to my car. I drive home and lie in bed for the next two days.

My heart doesn't break, it slips between my legs. I'm not sure if I'm being punished or if this is happening to test my character. Stan brings me flowers and stays home before returning to work. He is grieving too, but his grief is quiet, stoic, and hard.

I discover that you can eat your weight in chocolate and still not feel better and that the same holds true for salt and vinegar potato chips, easy mac extra cheese, and sugar cookies rolled in vanilla icing.

I don't care, just do something, anything, I beg the young Korean woman, who shrugs her shoulders and then aims the scissors at the back of my head. She snips soundlessly and I squeeze my eyes shut until she says, *all done* and even then I barely dare to look.

It is gone, all of it. My hair is cut close to the skull and I am happy. It is the desired effect.

I don't recognize myself at all.

Circle of Women

A circle of women put me back together when I am falling apart. I am stapled and glued and duct taped already, but they reinforce the attachments when everything I want in general and the babies, more specifically, fall apart. Sabot is a progressive preschool in a church basement run by Irene, a strong, nurturing, highly educated tiny redheaded woman with a PhD who hires me to look after tiny children, to play with them and support their play. Here I let myself be both caretaker and child.

The teachers at Sabot celebrate my engagement, bring desserts to my wedding, put flowers in my hair. Marty and Debbie and Sarah and Robin and Laura bring dinners and bags of groceries when the baby's heart stops beating. These women love me through learning how to play in the sandbox. They teach me to stop and eat snacks, to take a nap when I'm tired, to find hugs and shoulders and circles to lean in and on when I can't hold myself up alone.

Fiction Class

I am pregnant for the 6th time. I go to Reiki. I go to yoga. I pray. Two months pregnant, Stan gives me a fiction class at the Virginia Museum of Fine Arts. I haven't written in years. Not since college.

My writing died when I failed to produce an award-winning manuscript at graduation, on the dude ranch and the boat when I failed to write anything at all, with all the babies my body could not sustain.

I am now working part-time at Seven Hills, an all-boys middle school, in a church on north side. I don't know how to attach a document to an email but they hire me because I am friendly and enthusiastic and hit it off with the head of school who is a fantastic storyteller and a larger-than-life, gregarious guy.

I love the energy and fast pace of the school, but filing registration documents and taking attendance leaves me hungry. I am excited and scared to take a writing class, to find out if that part of me can be revived from the cold, dead earth. Can I be a student and a writer or am I stuck as secretary and wife? The class meets in the upstairs studio school of the art museum and at the large table of writers of various ages and occupations one man stands out.

Brandon is well over six feet tall and very young with spiky black hair and the face and mannerisms of a movie star. *Is that Ben Affleck?* The women writers gush when he goes to the bathroom. When he and I read our work out loud in class our eyes meet with a flash of recognition. We have both made up ridiculous worlds full of magic and mischief.

We have both written about mermaids.

That night in the parking lot we talk about writing, dreams, Gabriel García Márquez, his night job at Home Depot and his day job at the alternative paper, *Style Weekly. A real writer,* I think with admiration and envy. He emits his own light and heat. I want that, too.

Every Tuesday night for the next eight weeks my exhaustion and nausea lift like a fog over the mountain. Writing soaks into my skin like water. I excitedly type three pages of story that's workshopped in each class. Afterward in the parking lot, under the moon, Brandon and I talk about books and writing way past time to go home. He draws out a spark in me I thought had gone dark. I have a crush on Brandon but it isn't mutual. He is a tall, handsome man who believes in my writing and that makes a huge dumb difference to me.

The Wonder of That Moment

I almost stay at the office. There is so much filing to be done. Manila folders for each child in the school are spread across multiple folding tables begging to be organized before the new administrative assistant takes over the next day. *I don't think I can leave it like this,* I say to Stan on the phone.

Oh yes, you can, he says. *And you will. I'll be there in 10 minutes.* I haven't felt the baby move this morning. But it is my last day before maternity leave and I hate leaving so much work undone. I don't want to seem reactionary or hysterical. According to my schedule, I have three weeks left of pregnancy. Three weeks left to organize every single thing I possibly can before my life changes forever.

At the hospital, after monitoring his heart rate, the doctor cuts into me so fast blood splashes the faces of the attendants. My family races over and holds a prayer vigil in the lobby. The umbilical cord is wrapped three times around our baby's neck. They have to work fast.

While the doctors cut, I clutch a small, stuffed bear to my chest given to me by Santa, the Reiki practitioner who held her hands over me throughout the entire long, fearful, uncertain months of pregnancy. I knew the worst could happen, but I'd had moments of peace in her loving care.

Henry is born with his feet facing each other, his tiny toes clasped together like a monkey's, as if in prayer. My uterus, the doctors tell me, is heart-shaped, full of tumors, and it is a miracle the baby found space to grow there at all. After the terrifying, interminable minutes when they clear his lungs so he can breathe, he latches onto his father's nose, and then, at last, my nipple. I have never— and will never—get over the wonder of that moment.

I almost didn't leave work that day. I almost stayed behind to be a good girl, to tidy up, to get everything in order, to leave nothing undone. I didn't trust myself, I didn't listen to my body. My husband trusted my body more than I did and as much as I've learned, as far as we've come since then, I'll never be done thanking him for that.

A Person and a Parent

My son is born by emergency C-section during a maelstrom of miscarriages, three before and three after his birth. In the same few years, I had surgeries to remove an adrenal tumor, my gallbladder, fibroid tumors and eventually my uterus.

During this time, I'm not interested in self-care so much as sheer survival. Even though we are a nuclear family with one child and an excellent support system, a good day means wearing the shirt with the least breast milk on it and brushing my teeth every other day.

In addition to learning how to keep a tiny person alive, the week he is born I accept my first regular writing job at *Style* after leaving Seven Hills. So survival also means meeting my deadlines so I can stay out of jail or wherever they throw you when your book review is late and you're trying to decide which utility to keep this month.

I think of these first few years as being deep in the trenches, dodging enemy fire and projectile diarrhea. They are also precious, sweet, beautiful, fat-baby-with-milk-breath years, but my own level of personal self-care? Ha. Forget about it. I find myself slipping into a hazy mom-jean mode of the mind and body where I can no longer find the self I'd once known in my inner life or in the mirror.

It becomes apparent that I have to start taking care of not only my son's wants and needs, but my own—a statement that can still feel revolutionary and selfish and risky and shot through with truth, written down.

Luckily I'm also an alcoholic and the resulting recovery groups I attend remind me that when the plane's going down I have to put the oxygen mask on myself first. I have to learn to focus on my physical, mental, emotional, and spiritual well-being frequently or this whole family unit is going to nose dive, crash land, and burst into flames.

But what does taking care of myself mean exactly? It's a gradual process of discovery. At first, I thought it meant eating as many donuts as I wanted while getting a mani/pedi—and it can mean that—but it's deeper and bigger, too.

It's repeatedly asking this one radical question posed to me by a wise friend: *What's the most loving thing I can do for myself right now?* The answer varies wildly from a hot bath to journaling to going on a retreat to praying to stopping to breathe to asking for help. The answer always comes if I'm patient enough to listen.

Re-reading a journal from a few years ago, I find a letter I'd written to my son who accused me of being more of a person than a parent. I've found his comment both heartbreaking and affirming—both then and now.

Of course, I think most mothers strive to be both—but God forbid that your child notices! *I have wanted you my entire life—more than you could ever know,* I wrote to him in my journal. *My deepest hope is that I can help you learn how to become fully and completely yourself by becoming fully and completely myself, too.*

I'd rather show him the importance of living a big, beautiful, creative life through the power of example than by the power of breathing down his neck and telling him what to do.

As I integrate self-care more fully into my life, I hope to pass on to him a blueprint of how to take the best possible care of himself—whether or not he becomes a parent one day, too.

Home Free

After his traumatic birth, I feel I should be allowed to revel in the exquisite life of my beautiful baby without intervention, illness, or trauma. We deserve to be home-free. When the pediatrician tells me my baby has positional club feet because of my heart-shaped uterus, I am furious. My baby has to have his tiny legs and ankles set in casts and then wear corrective medical shoes that turn his ankles in opposite directions for months after that.

I weep and he screams as they wrap his fat little legs in plaster. My perfect baby looks like he has two broken legs. The casts are heavy and restrict movement. One day poop leaks from his diaper and seeps into the plaster thighs; I can't scrub it out.

While visiting Stan's mother in North Carolina, Henry starts to sneeze and wheeze and I check his temperature every 10 minutes. I sit in the backseat and nurse him in my arms the five-hour ride home praying not to get a ticket because I can't bear to let him scream in his car seat alone.

The next morning the pediatrician checks his vital signs and says he needs to be admitted to the hospital immediately. He has walking pneumonia and RSV and needs IVs and an oxygen tank. He is hooked up to tubes in an incubator, still with casts on his tiny legs. He looks like he barely survived a four-car pileup. I sleep in the bed next to him for a week and read and cry and pray.

Can We Talk?

Can we turn off the TV and talk? I ask. I always want to ask this. We lie side by side, in silence, and now I can't think of anything to say.

What is marriage anyway? What task does it perform? What good does it do? What purpose does it serve? My husband has a logical mind and he finds this line of questioning ridiculous. I ask too much and want too much, more than anyone can give.

I'm here for you, Stan says. *But this isn't the 17th century where we sit around staring into each other's eyes by candlelight for entertainment. Maybe I should move to Europe and then we can write each other letters every few months.*

Can we? I ask. That sounds like a good idea to me.

There Are Days

The sky is full and heavy like a big pregnant cow. Each muscle in my neck is tender and tight like swollen roots under the earth. The clouds have lent me a mask that I wear like a mink around my neck and over my head, pinching, a clasp too transparent to break.

There are days when I feel ugly and poor and dirty and broke and I'm dragging myself through a cesspool of quicksand. I lose my keys, accidentally hit myself in the face, bite my tongue, step on my own toe, rip my page, lose my place and hate everyone, most of all me.

Two Bulls

In the spring of 2008, during the height of the financial crisis, I am laid off from my desk job at *Style Weekly* along with many other writers and staff, each one walking the plank into the publisher's office, aware we are facing certain doom. Stan has just quit his job at Audio Exchange in order to start his own business and now neither one of us has health insurance. We fight about money all of the time like two bulls with our horns locked in combat.

All of my safety nets have been stripped away. I feel naked and raw and vulnerable and angry. I cry through my recovery meetings and while I watch Henry play, terrified of what could happen were he to get hurt in any way. I can barely afford to buy sunscreen at Target. I feel like a negligent and irresponsible mother. Every expense is formidable. I stop answering the phone, and my bills pile up in drawers, the seals of the envelopes unbroken.

The Path

I don't tell my husband about the phone call. I keep it hidden, a guilty secret. The rabbi who channels a mystic named Sam welcomes me into his meticulous house. I have to write an article about him for my column in *Belle*, a local women's magazine, but the truth is, I desperately need his advice. *Am I on the right path?* He doesn't exactly answer my question, but he does give me an answer I can interpret any way I want, like a fortune cookie.

There are no wrong paths on the road of life—or something like that. I've asked point-blank if it is insane to choose a life of writing over a full-time job, but apparently, it doesn't work that way. Sam doesn't give direct answers to direct questions.

The rabbi is a short, sweet man, and as I leave his house I know I will eventually have to come clean to my husband about turning down the offer of a full-time job with benefits copywriting for a credit card company just a few weeks after our internet is shut off. We have no health insurance, we're eating too many rice and beans, and new clothes are only a dream.

But I want to write. I *need* to write. I can't imagine long days crammed into a box, even a box that comes with a paycheck. And so I say *no* on the phone call that could have been salvation, a way out, the key to saving the family from ruin. I carry the weight like a criminal until I fess up, finally come clean, and tell Stan the truth.

I've chosen my path. The path with my name on it. Not the quickest or easiest path. Not the shortcut to money or security or success. I close one door and a million others open. Sometimes they open slowly, but they do open. Saying no to that job was the best no I ever said.

The Thing I Want to Do Forever

I piece together every freelance writing and teaching gig I can, but it is not enough. I'm serving on the board of the James River Writers, a nonprofit for writers, where I lead workshops and moderate panels when Virginia, the director, asks if I know of any creative writing camps for kids. *I'm so sorry, I don't,* I tell her. And then, when she asks me again I volunteer to teach her son and a couple of his friends myself.

While I'm writing down my dreams for the class I realize there must be a better place to hold class than Virginia's attic. I ask Ward at Chop Suey Books if I can rent the art gallery on the second floor of his shop and he says, *sure.* I learn how to set up a free website on Blogger and borrow folding tables from a friend.

I reach out to the authors I've met through *Style Weekly*, asking them to be guest teachers at my camp, and then all of the families I know to see if their kids want to sign up. That summer I teach my first four weeks of Richmond Young Writers, and it is miraculous. I feel the same deep connection and spark of creative writing utopia I felt when I was a kid at camp myself.

The next fall I begin teaching creative nonfiction classes for adults at the Black Swan Bookshop where Brandon and I held a writing group on Tuesday nights for the last five years. The owners graciously allow me use of their space to teach in the evenings. Even though the income is small, driving home after my first class I know I have found the thing I want to do for the rest of my life.

Darkness

Stan's darkness becomes visceral. It emanates. You can feel it when you walk into the room. Not darkness so much as an absence of light, absence of *anything*. When times are hard for me, when I'm triggered or wrestling grief, I act out. He shuts down. I get bigger and louder. He gets small and silent. His depression infuriates me. Please please please *get up*. Please do *something. Anything.*

After his father dies in our second year of marriage, he stops sleeping. Even sleeping pills don't help him sleep. When the babies die and my body is in shock and surgery and recovery and the only time we touch is when he helps change my bandages, he pushes down his sorrow and rage while mine explodes out, splattering everything.

I've always been afraid of abandonment, but I didn't think I could feel abandoned with my husband right here in the house, sleeping or watching TV. I want to jump on him and punch him and shake him but when I yell for him to come closer, he goes further away. Henry is the one person for whom he can act alive.

My husband doesn't leave me, but sometimes I wish he would. I turn to my work, to the page, to the computer, to the sudden spark of life I find there, that makes me primed, easy prey.

Love Language

I consider myself someone with a high emotional IQ and Stan's basically a genius so how is it that we are both so dumb? Misunderstandings, misinterpretations, words thrown out that don't meet in the middle. We don't speak the same language or come from the same planet. What oh what oh what have I done?

And then I have a dream that Stan is my *Spiritual Husband*. That we are psychically linked together in order to grow. I remember the dream about running a marathon together long before he even asked me out on our first date. If we can't always talk in real life, I get powerful messages about him in dreams.

After a fight, I tell Stan I don't think we know each other's love languages anymore.

I think your love language is fighting, he says and it is a gently placed punch to the gut.

Domestic Life

It's 55 degrees in the house. I can see my breath. We have no money to fix the heater. Stan takes my coldness personally. I put on gloves to hide my despair.

Doing dishes is a long slog up a tall mountain. Laundry is hands and knees across the desert. My husband is a piece of furniture that sometimes talks, moves. I have to unearth single spoons from beneath the acre of dirty dishes to stir my coffee. The laundry molds in the machine.

I resent the life I have created so I try to ignore it.

I withdraw from the family. I have to pump life into the self I have abandoned. I create Bad Valley and then live through her vicariously. She's made entirely of words at first but she starts to take shape and form in little actions that give her more of me than I'd bargained for.

Trickster and Dominatrix

He contacts me the first time after I write an article about the book, *I Was a Teenage Dominatrix*, which includes an interview with the author, now a professor in her 40s. *What can you tell me about dominatrixes?* he asks in a private message. I am flattered to see his name on my screen. He intimidates and impresses me so I tell him the truth. I know nothing about dominatrixes except what I've read in the book. He is welcome to read it, too.

The conversation doesn't stop there. He pushes me and presses me and I respond, pressing and pushing back. We fight over what he considers my misuse of the word *semantics*. We fight over the definition of the word *discipline*. And then, what was at first playful banter becomes an involved game of role-play, in which he encourages me to dominate and humiliate him, a task I find surprisingly easy to do. But it isn't always satisfying for me, and this point is driven home by the flush in my cheeks every time we talk. We only use words on screens that aren't real even though they crawl through my flesh. And when I see his name pop up on my screen, I shut the door to my office.

One day when my husband sees an open chat box and asks, *Who's that?* I turn crimson. *It's just a friend,* I say. *We're just talking.*

But I know how much talking means to you, my husband says. Soon though, it isn't just talking. It is photographs and videos, too. Our conversations become so elaborate and involved that my real life begins to feel like my pretend life and my pretend life feels far too real.

I tell my therapist it feels like I'm 1000 pieces of dried-up paper and he's thrown a match. *Hmmm,* my therapist says. *I think you alone were ready to burn.*

Why does it feel like I am salvaging the best and most interesting parts of myself when I type words on a screen to a man who is brilliant and devious and can also be truly cruel in order to rile me up to punish him more? He tells me I'm just another housewife writing for the local rag. He is interested in my friends. He drives me insane. And I can't stop writing to him. I quit a thousand times and always return. I've started smoking again, too, and I can't quit that either. Crouching behind the dumpster in our backyard with a cigarette feels like *living.*

One of my friends says she sees me descending after him into hell, a bride of the devil. She performs a ceremony at Poe's graveyard in Baltimore where she and I are doing a reading together, severing the black ribbon wound between us. *I have to end this,* he tells me the very next day. *It's too much like a drug, like heroin.*

I try to turn our story into a manuscript and share the first 50 pages with my oldest friend, Sarah. *This would make the New York Times bestseller list,* she tells me. *Too bad you can never publish it.* And she is right. I can never publish it. I can't even finish it. My obsession eclipses everything. When Stan finds video clips on my computer, he asks me to pack a bag and leave the house. *This is emotional abuse,* he says. I walk across the street to my mother's house sobbing. She takes me in without judgment or recrimination, silently handing me a checklist of questions to determine whether or not I am addicted to sex and love. The list is like a mirror that cracks in two as I read.

The Dog Door

I crawl through the dog door to get back into my house after Stan locks me out. I would leave him if I had the money but I am broke, which my mother says is a blessing like in the story of the girls in the concentration camp who thanked God for the fleas and then they were passed over and able to escape because the guards who didn't want to become flea-infested, too. Stan accepts my return but is silent and cold.

I've just read my little boy *Hush Little Dragon* and I sob through every refrain, wondering how a mother can read a book to a child she might not be waking up next to in the morning. I feel sick and diseased and branded. And I am, with shame and a home in the swamp where I've rented out my heart. Pawned it. Traded it in for fool's gold that turned out to be a big pile of trash.

My husband is never cruel, or excited by emotional hostage-taking or verbal sword fights. Those are the weapons of the online affair I'm unbinding myself from.

Release

We have marriage counseling and I'm dreading it. After our last session I cried in my car for ten minutes even though Stan told me later he thought counseling was awesome. *How else are we going to get the shit out and let ourselves heal?* he asks. I thought that after all these years of marriage I'd know more instead of less. My parents both got married more than once and my primal internal clock says surely our time is up, too. But then it's not and it's not, it's the middle of our life, the middle of our marriage.

I want a big, expansive life and Stan wants the life we already have. He's content with not changing anything. Sitting still drives me out of my mind while moving forward seems unnecessary to him. I want action, drama, excitement, adventure. He wants quiet, peace, stability. We're stuck in the middle, moving in different directions. Is it wrong to not just want what you want but to want the person you're married to, to want more, too?

Everything I Thought I Knew

I sit in my meditation nook and hold myself until I can feel some part of my self return. Stan and Henry had a fight and I made myself walk away, unable to untangle their web without spinning 20 more of my own. *Maybe I'm incapable of having intimate personal relationships, I think. Maybe they're just not meant to be.*

I've always been able to get close up, wind tight, get so connected it's as if neither of us had separate skin. But those relationships have been unraveling one by one and I feel more naked, colder, more anxious, more alone than ever in my life. I'm having to rely less on the God I thought I knew and more on a God who is changing right before my eyes.

I am having to rely more on myself.

I take a beautiful handmade notebook from my window that I've been saving since my birthday. I begin to write things I know to be true. *You're lovable and capable of loving even if it doesn't feel like it,* and *everything sucks right now but your heart is made of pure love,* and so on.

In the distance, I can hear Henry say *sorry* and Stan says *sorry* back, and I know their drama is done. So simple and so complete. After a few more minutes I join them to watch bad TV and when the show is over Stan turns it off.

Let's all talk about our feelings, he says and it hits me that by sitting quietly with my feelings, the webs unknotted all by themselves. This is new for me. This is rocket science. I am re-learning everything I thought I knew.

Tectonic Plates

Do you really want to leave me or do you just need to eat breakfast? I ask Stan after a shift in the tectonic plates. It's a stupid fight but it's escalated quickly.

I don't think this is working out, he says.

What the fuck what the fuck what the fuck do you mean?

Henry and a friend are running in and out of the room spying on us with a periscope Henry made at camp last week. I keep waiting for him to laugh, to take it back, to say he's joking. But he doesn't.

I get that desperate breaking feeling inside when the cracks are too big to hold. I beg, I plead, I tell him he can't go back to work until we are resolved. He stays. We patch it up, hug. I feel relief floods, waves of gratitude. Our marriage is full of duct tape, superglue, tissues we shove in the cracks. But later it comes unstuffed once again. The center spills out all over again, messy and old. Some words can't be tossed about carelessly and then written back in, swallowed, eaten. They spark and stay, gouging out leveled earth once so firmly packed in.

At the marriage counselor, Stan says, *I want to divorce Valley so that we can start dating again.* Sometimes when I see the word marriage it's like looking through a mummy's gauze, a funhouse mirror. I don't know what it is I see.

Shack Martha Stewart

When I get home from teaching, ready for bed and bad TV, Stan starts to sand the kitchen ceiling. From my position under the covers, I can see white specks of sheetrock begin to coat the pots and pans hanging from their hooks, the stovetop and burners (minus the one that caught on fire that we threw into the backyard the night before), the baskets of apples Henry and I picked at the orchard, the cat food, the coffee maker and every other conceivable surface within 100 feet, including Stan himself.

I get up for a bowl of store-brand granola with expensive organic whole milk and pad across the plywood floor we let our son draw on with a sharpie until we get our REAL floor—that mythical unicorn of bourgeois renovation I've heard plenty about but am not sure will ever actually materialize. My footprints are visible behind me as if I have just tracked across a pristine sandy beach on a tropical island. I pour my granola, resolve not to say a word and pretend instead that we live in the out of doors. On a beach. In a snowstorm. God forbid I impede progress.

Because our house—like our mental health and our marriage—is nothing if not a work in progress. The front porch, living room, backyard, kitchen, bathroom, bedroom, and tool shed, all under different states of construction. Merge this with my thwarted longing to craft, an allergic reaction to cleaning, a deep inner desire to hostess, and an almost primal urge to feed people and make them feel at home—even in a home in which I feel at turns like a queen and the beggar on her knees outside the castle.

In one of my 12 step meetings, I sob, *I want to have it all together but I just can't! Everything is such a mess. I am Shack Martha Stewart!*

Sarah suggests I start a new line of items for the home available exclusively at the Dollar Tree. *I-Tried-to-Clean-But-Couldn't* air freshener. *Too-Bad-We-Only-Have-Four-Places-to-Sit* placemats. *Whoops!-I-Burnt-the-Hell-Out-of-Dinner* after-dinner mints. I could even make *Turn Your Hovel into Home* DIY videos based on scavenger hunts through the attic for art to hang on the walls and the arrangement of potted plants almost guaranteed not to die. Truly, they do wonders. We named ours Plant A, Plant B, and Bob.

A Thing of Real Beauty

Most of our neighbors have been around since before I was born–
Frank and Fran who go to Dollywood every summer. Ed who drives
a big rig when he's not working at the Exxon station.

In the rental to our right are the transients—Jack who calls his dog
Goddamnit and asks me to spy on his wife who moved out one
weekend while he was gone, and then Trinity the single mom, next
a bodybuilder with a red sports car, license plate *SO RAD,* and now
our neighbors who love NASCAR and football and run bingo night
at the Gay thrift store.

Our house has the same holly bushes with red berries surrounding
the front porch it's always had, but our purple shutters are new,
ours alone.

We had our front porch re-tiled. The elegant design of the four different
patterns of blue and white tiles is a thing of real beauty. It took
many years in this house for me to care about it. I'd wanted to live
anywhere but here, anywhere but in my skin, with anyone but
myself. I don't know if we will move or if we will stay. The answer

to that question changes every time I ask it. But I'm ready to take away the broken parts, to fix what I can, to make it as beautiful as possible, while we're still here.

This House

There are pictures of me in this house from when I was a baby, with my parents in rooms that are like other countries in distant lands. I'm standing naked in my mother's cowboy boots. I am crawling naked up the cement back steps. My mom and dad cradle me in their arms on the front porch. He has a mustache. Her hair is long. They are so young and gorgeous and they will stay together forever and the house will not disintegrate around them.

There are photographs of my dad in cut-off jean shorts and a bandana building the shed out back before he forgot how tools work. There's my mother's art studio where we made lampshades and she painted the fired clay dug up from our own backyard. There's a photo of me with my hair permed wearing turquoise eyeshadow and a sequined turquoise dress for the eighth-grade sock hop. There are pictures of me lying on the couch reading underneath armfuls of cats.

If you go through the pictures you'll find photographs of a million different cultures and colors, entire lands and distant kingdoms come and gone, all on the same plot of land that held first my parents, and then my own family, and me.

One Day I'll Tell You

I yell at my husband for leaving all of his tools and electronics and boxes of wire from his truck on the couches in our living room for 5 days straight. I believe I will be absolved in a court of law of any crime I have to commit in order to restore order to my own house. But then Henry says, *One day I'll tell you how much I hate it when you two fight,* and my stomach becomes a hard rock sinking to the bottom of the sea.

I text my husband *I'm sorry I was an asshole* and he texts that he is sorry back. At dinner, I point out to our son that at least when we fight we get over it quickly unlike some people who never fight but silently hate each other for years.

Dinner is delicious and I even wear a frilly apron and smile with true pleasure all while the mounds and piles in the living room stand their ground. After the storm passes I can ignore them with ease. The mess becomes part of the beauty of life.

For Better and Worse

On Sunday when the motor of the MG explodes oil all over the walls and the cement floor of the shed like blood from a gutted body, Stan takes to bed. He cannot be roused.

Imagine you lost the hard drive with your book on it, he says to me but I don't want to make the comparative leap. Half of me has compassion and half of me wants to scream *get out of fucking bed, man!* But my husband's heart belongs to boats and cars and motors and engines the way my heart belongs to words.

We speak different languages and love different things but even at our worst, he has the primal smell of the man I married. I want to throttle him and he's who I turn to for the biggest and smallest things. Marriage is not what I ever imagined it would be. It is far better and it's also far worse.

Just What I Always Wanted

They come on like thunder, volcanic eruptions, fugue states. Afterward, I'm exhausted and emptied out, like a drainpipe after a heavy storm. I wish I could go away for a couple of months and scream and yell and smash things until all of the rage has left my system so I can return home feeling sweet and clean. But it's not happening that way. I'm erupting in geysers of rage in my own home, at my own family. It's killing us.

The other day Stan told Henry he promised never to hurt him physically but made no promises about mentally or emotionally. All of us laughed. We laugh a lot. We are healing. We are healing so much. But I know the scars in the psyche formed pre-memory. All of those fights. All of that yelling. The rage rising up in me, steam from a geyser, lava through a volcano, as natural and unstoppable as a natural disaster.

Henry says that Stan should care more and that I should care less. When I try to get Stan to do what I think he should do, those fights are the most hopeless of all. When there's a death or loss we hold each other and talk and talk ourselves through.

Henry used to open every single present he received by breaking into a huge grin and exclaiming, *It's just what I always wanted!* Even if he had no idea what it was. When he'd climb out of the bathtub I'd roll him up in a towel like a burrito and hand him over to his father. *It's just what I always wanted!* Stan would say, holding him tight in his arms.

How to Survive Hard Feelings

One day after dropping Henry off at preschool, my mother calls me. *I just want you to know,* she says, *Henry's teacher told me what he shared at Circle Time yesterday. 'Daddy said bad words and mommy slammed the door.'*

Oh fuck, I say. We already make most of our school payments late, some months we barely pay the mortgage and we have no health insurance at all. We've been fighting over who's doing what and who could do more. Neither of us has enough time to work or enough money to pay for childcare. Now I'll have to pull Henry out of school altogether. Not from poverty but from shame. How can I ever face his teacher again? She is patient, wise, kind, and loving. She would never slam the fucking door.

But the next morning, Marty greets me with a loving smile. *It's OK for children to see their parents fight,* she tells me. *That's how they learn they can survive hard feelings. We have to model it for them.*

I cry with relief at her kindness. And I hope to God she's right.

Garbage Disposal

I see that my husband has dumped a barrel of trash into our backyard. *It was full of water,* he says.

But now our yard is full of trash, I say.

I'll clean it up, he says and he does, but I'm already mad. *How can this be the man I married?* I seethe. Until at night when he coaxes our rescue dog in from the back yard, wet and shivering, towels her off, rubs her belly, and strokes her ears, until she grunts her strange alien purr, and he nuzzles his face into her neck and I think. *Ok. Yes. THIS is the man I married.*

Inside of my one marriage, I feel like two distinct people. When I'm the one person I can't imagine the thoughts or emotions or reasons behind the other.

And then the other me comes out. The me that has been crushed and wronged, that is underwater and can't see the surface, that feels misunderstood, discounted, and full of rage. The me that wants to fight, lash out, and leave.

I'm trying to nail down the switch that flips me from one into the other and then back again. I'm trying to discover how I can eclipse the side of myself that wants me miserable and dead with the side that laughs hard, forgives easily, and sees the light.

This weekend after many beautiful days strung together like prayer flags on a clothesline, I feel another storm moving in. I meditate and journal and go to a yoga class. I sweat and sob and let me move through me. When I return home the driving rain has turned into a quiet drizzle.

I pray and ask for help and try not to pick a fight just to let off steam.

I sit with myself until I pass on through.

You're the Asshole

Mary Kay, my pastor friend, and I are walking up and down the rolling hills of her suburban neighborhood. We are wearing yoga pants and I have on a new fanny pack. We each have a dog at the end of a leash, poop bags tied in a knot at the ready. I am crying. Again. I feel like there's a boa constrictor in my belly squeezing my guts into knots. *All he wants to do is watch TV*, I say. *I'm cooking, I'm cleaning, I'm trying to do things outside of our little prison and he just wants to watch garbage and nap. He is such an asshole!* I yell this a little louder than her quiet suburban streets call for.

She stops dead in her tracks. She puts her arm on my elbow and swivels me around until I am facing her. *Maybe he's just tired*, Valley, she says. *Maybe you're the asshole.*

Her words pop the tight thing in my chest. The constrictor reconfigures.

I'm the asshole? I ask.

Yeah, maybe he needs to decompress and get some rest and you won't let him.

I'm the asshole, I say again, trying it without a question mark this time. Just as we start walking again my dog takes a poop on the curb. I bag it and taste the words expanding in my mouth. I start to laugh. If I'm the asshole, I can try *not* to be an asshole. *There's hope,* I say.

Exactly, she says. *If you're the asshole there's hope. Maybe you should go home, climb into bed with him and watch trash TV together.*

And that's exactly what I do.

Shadow Year

Stan whispers in my ear *there's no one I'd rather be miserable with than you.* Is this love? *Fuck.* But for us, for now, it is.

In the last week or so we have felt closer, we have talked and listened and spent time together like two adults who are able to be more than miserable. Friday night he suggested we go to the Virginia Museum which delighted me as he is an introverted homebody usually happiest going nowhere, talking to no one.

At the museum, Stan takes a selfie in front of Edward Munch's line drawing of a vulva. And Stan never takes selfies. Jasper Johns' work doesn't interest me at all but Munch's drawings of angst, despair, illness, sex, and death fascinate me. I feel at home in those harrowing depictions of the dark side—one a self-portrait of himself literally in the fires of hell.

Now that I'm not drinking or eating myself to death, I can put a buffer between myself and the abyss, and sometimes it wears thin. I've been having a lot of filmy darkness hanging in and over and around, the kind that stops me from leaping out of bed, that makes me force myself up and out and through my day. I'm getting rid of a lot of bad stuff but getting rid of it feels bad. One of my favorite phrases has always been *wretched excess*. I'd like to live in the swampy ocean of too much of everything.

This year I can look back and see as if it were a drawing or a map, the lines reforming between myself and everyone I know. Each tightened or severed thread has come with pain before release. I had a tarot card reading with Archana and she said that this was my shadow year, a year of pulling up the tree I've been hacking from the roots. I can't say I wasn't warned.

Reflexes

When Henry gets off the bus he accidentally crumples the tinfoil ship he made with my mom last night. As it sags further he smashes it in a fit of rage and then I get mad at him for getting mad at his ship. When we get home Stan yells at both of us for being angry and yelling at each other.

Prayers prayers prayers are said. Within an hour we are talking about reflexes, Henry's reflex to smash things, my reflex to get mad at him for being mad, Stan's reflex to try to fix the whole thing by making it worse.

While we talk Henry makes a new tinfoil ship out of the old one with tiny figures on board staring out at the big wide sea.

Hero's Journey

At my doctor's appointment, I finally talk to my nurse practitioner, an Amazon of a woman with a shock of silver hair. I tell her about my anxiety. Waking up in a panic, pounding heart, racing thoughts. How hard it's been to get out of bed. The lethargy, the exhaustion. The self-incriminating thoughts. The inability to stop crying. That last symptom I demonstrate generously throughout our conversation. My history of addiction, my family's history with addiction, and depression, and anxiety. How I've tried to self-medicate. I think I'm ready for chemical help, I say through tears. We go through the checklist of things I should do first. Do I exercise? Yes. Meditate? Yes. Journal? Yes.

I think you're absolutely right, she says. *You're on a hero's journey and you need to gather together all of your forces.*

Can a hero still take antidepressants? I asked.

Oh hell yes, she says and writes me a script I fill that night.

Big Beautiful Life

I stand in my living room and scream at my husband at the top of my lungs: *I'M GOING TO HAVE A BIG BEAUTIFUL LIFE WHETHER YOU WANT TO OR NOT!*

I used to long and pine and beg my husband to seek help and go on meds. The truth is I honestly thought that if he got on meds, I would feel better. And then I was interrogated by some very wise and direct people who had the nerve to ask if I was happy. Was I on meds? How were they working for me? Had I found the answer? Had I found joy?? When I finally decided to accept psychiatric help I began to create the big beautiful life I'd been yelling at him about.

As I add more and more modalities into my own personal plan for happiness and healing, my theme is expansion. My heart and spirit are expanding. My classes and retreats and press and literary community are expanding. Even my hips are expanding! We are putting our house on the market and expanding out of my childhood home. I don't have to make my husband go anywhere. I have to learn to go there myself.

On the Boat Again

We have rented a houseboat tied to a dock for the weekend. It is blissful, even when I'm sure the boat is too far away from the dock to jump, even though we have to walk to the bathhouse for serious bathroom needs in the pouring rain, even though it is tinier than any of our tiny bedrooms, I love everything about it. We all do.

Walking down the road well before 7 AM, I faceplant in the asphalt, phone in one hand, cup of coffee in the other. When I peel my head up I see a man with a handlebar mustache rushing towards me. *You know you're old when people stop laughing at you when you fall,* Stan says, but I appreciate this man's firm grip even while wishing the earth will swallow me whole.

Mom, you're covered in blood and sand and coffee, Henry says, and we walk to the river to wash me off. I laugh so hard that I start crying even harder, bruised and bloodied elbow-knee-pinkie finger, coffee in my hair and down my dress, gravel and sand all over, but the river washes me clean, absorbs the brunt of my fall.

Imprint

Have I turned fat and ugly? I ask my husband.

Are you stupid? he asks back. His is a fair question. He has always adored even the ugliest parts of me.

Just wondering, I say and then I start to cry.

Come here, he says and hugs me hard. *You're still the beautiful woman I married.*

I am and I'm not. Life transforms us. And whether we want to or not, it's impossible to remain the people we were before we were the imprint of the other.

Extraordinary Love

Today I wake up with the thought, *I expect extraordinary love from an ordinary man.* I want to be loved the way God loves Jesus, the way the devil loves hell. In fact, I don't even want love, I want worship.

I read once in the aptly but horrifically titled book *Emotional Incest* that the favorite child of divorced parents, the one showered with love, attention, and laser focus, swept off her feet with indulgence and fun, can never be loved enough again. The parent is the child's god and the adult version of that child will never find his equal. This sounds like such a good problem to have compared to abuse or neglect but my therapist points out it's like being served chocolate for every meal. It's too much. The center cannot hold.

Loving too much is a sneaky, nasty drug, one that can look just like kindness, compassion, and care but will bleed you dry until suddenly you're empty and starving.

What is marriage for, again?

What is marriage for again? I ask my sponsor. Again.

To make us conscious, she says, again. She has told me this 1,000 times. I want her to say something different. To make us happy. To make us rich. To make us whole. So we will be saved.

She refuses to say any of that.

We've been married nearly two decades and I may be beginning to form my own answers. I've wanted my husband to save me once, a thousand times. A few years ago, every time I heard the word marriage I felt like I was bound and gagged in Saran Wrap. I felt thunderstruck by the idea that if things went *well,* I would never have another first kiss again. Now I feel like marriage is an anchor that keeps me tethered to this earth.

He refuses to save me.

I can't believe we've made it this far, Stan says to me. *I don't even like people.*

No kidding, I say. In all fairness, I lean on him in a million invisible ways every day. I thought marriage would be more of a linear trajectory but instead, it's an arena filled with battles, surrender, forgiveness, and other impossible things.

Minimum Requirement

My son's teacher, Mrs. X—fast-paced and gorgeous—is in her mid-twenties and has more energy than a golden retriever. *Your son,* she tells us, *is very bright. He's making straight As. But he's figured out how to do only what's required of him and nothing more. He's figured out the minimum requirement.*

Oh God, says my husband who looks like he hasn't gotten a haircut in 3 years. *That's all I ever heard in school. That I wasn't living up to my potential. That's me to a T.*

And how old were you when you stopped doing the minimum requirement? asks Mrs. X, staring at him pointedly.

What time is it now? asks my husband, looking down at an imaginary watch. My husband, who dropped out of college, is halfway through renovating our kitchen, plumbing the bathroom, and digging out a new driveway.

And there I am, terrified for the future of my bright boy who is in the 3rd grade making straight As. All the boys I've ever loved before him—genius level, fucked up underachievers flash before my eyes. How do I get my son to want to do more than the minimum requirement when that's all we do ourselves? When he's already announced he'd rather be homeschooled and live on an island off the grid never paying taxes? When sometimes, we need to have a chance to take a break and do nothing at all?

What Could be More Important Than This?

I have a lot to do, but Henry wants to go to the park, so I take him to Cheswick, just a mile from our house. He runs through the paths finding objects of nature to arrange into compositions that he can photograph and that I can sketch. At one point we cross the creek and he bounds across with a perfect combination of safety and confidence.

I feel totally at odds with my body on wet shifting rocks so I cross on all fours like a wild animal. I feel foolish but glad not to be too landlocked to follow him at all. He is the leader with an eye for each shot he wants, great rotting logs leaning at precarious angles into the water, a dead turtle, a gumball held wet in his hand, his little face peering brightly through a rotted-out stump.

What could be more important than this? I'm sure millions of parents before me, who suddenly find themselves in the middle of the woods with a child who is still able to see and love each individual tree, have wondered this, too.

God

At family dinner we let Henry say the prayer—Henry, who says he'd like to be a druid and if he were to have a bar mitzvah he would say *nature! nature! I'm a man!* For the blessing, he tells a story about a banana who likes to ride a bicycle and when he's done we say *amen!*

Every Sunday morning at my recovery meeting, God speaks through stories of resurrection and life after life, men and women coming back from the dead, lives plundered and ruined and then rebuilt and relived and I feel my own God in my own story and it's enough to have and to have quietly without pomp or circumstance.

Last year I fret about giving Henry no religion, no Sunday school, no frame of reference for either Testament. Should we go to church or synagogue? I ask him. *Neither, Mom,* he says. *Just go to one of your meetings.* And I do.

Prey

This morning I wake to loud expressive crunching right outside my door and I'm afraid my girl cat, Sun, is eating another bunny severed in half, organs scattered across the floor. But it is only my dog Virginia eating a generous portion of nachos Henry abandoned the night before. And just as the relief sinks in, I see it—the naked featherless baby bird—alien in its translucent, tiny and perfect embryonic state. What do I do with my vicious killer when I love her so much?

The night before I snuggled Sun and our bearded dragon in my arms at the same time reveling in the joy of their embrace. After eating all the kale he could off the perch of my chest the dragon leaped off of me onto and over the cat who startled, much more accustomed to hunting prey than being trampled by it.

That night I dream my mother has a lion cub swaddled in a baby blanket rocking gently in her lap, the soft soft fur an alarming contrast to the brilliant gleam of the sharp white fangs.

When I was little I dreamed lions ran free in our neighborhood and was terrified to leave the screened-in front porch playing ship, ocean, mermaid, and pogo stick from the safety of the cement steps as often as I could. The cars that drove by were the sharks and the people were the fish and the grass was a forest of seaweed in my underwater ocean world and though I loved the lions I felt their danger, knew they lurked above, stalking me, on dry land.

Eat It

On a Sunday night, Henry, Stan, and I drive to Wolftrap Center for
the Performing Arts to see *Weird Al Yankovic's Mandatory Fun
World Tour.* As soon as we get there Henry looks down at his NASA
t-shirt and then up at the hundreds and thousands of white
people wearing math, science, calculus, Star Wars, The Simpsons,
Lord of the Rings, Pokémon, and physics t-shirts and he says, *Oh
no, I'm a stereotype. Look, Mom!* The couple behind us is eating their
picnic on a blanket of the periodic table.

I see my past, present, and future selves all here, he says. And he points
them out as we look around.

Weird Al was your first concert, I say the afternoon after his fourth
day of middle school, that ring of hell that makes even strong men
shudder. *What would you like your second concert to be?*

Weird Al, he says and we laugh and I feel like I know weird Al
intimately because he's the background pop culture of my entire life
and we listened to a 90-minute podcast with him on the way up.

I cried during Weird Al, Stan admits the next day. *I was just so happy we were all there together as a family.* And I know what he means. We'd had another earth-shattering fight the night before and we'd both wondered if our foundation could hold the weight of such terrible rumbling.

To lie on a blanket and look at the sky with the two people you love more than anything can make your heart ache and break with tenderness and joy. And to do so while a brilliant nerd in a fat suit sings *Eat It* is a pretty major lifetime achievement.

Werewolf Bar Mitzvah

Henry turns 13 on Saturday. Stan sets up an obstacle course in the backyard involving pulleys and ladders, any insurance adjuster's worst nightmare. The kids have to solve riddles, break codes, open locks, and work together to get through the brilliant Jerry rigged puzzle of Stan's devious mind. They love it. We have tacos and pumpkin cake and the boys set up a tent with lanterns and sleeping bags and glow in the dark fake bloody fingers and bouncy eyeballs.

We invite a couple of family friends over, make a fire pit and sing the songs you sing at night with people you love. After the expected birthday traditions are over Henry comes to me and says, *Mom, I want to have a Bar Mitzvah. Go get my Burger King crown from the car.* So I find it squashed up in the back of the trunk and follow his instructions. *I'll get on the trampoline and you'll crown me,* he says and everyone gathers around in a circle as he bends down on one knee and I place the crown on his head.

Hallelujah! he shouts and everyone cheers and we listen to Tracy Morgan's *Werewolf Bar Mitzvah* and now I'm the mother of a teenager and every day is a new unexpected world. I certainly never expected these days to be so good. I didn't think much past his birth, getting him here alive absorbed every ounce of imagination I had. For his birthday he's asked for a briefcase and a hoodie from the ACLU. He wants to carry the briefcase instead of a backpack and perhaps someday soon he will. The balancing act, the unbelievable transformation from boy to man.

What We're Able
and Unable to Do

Earlier this week Henry came home from school a few minutes later than usual. *Was the bus late?* I asked.

No, he said. *I stopped to call the county to report a stop sign that fell at Hillside and Granger.*

You did? I asked. I would have walked by that stop sign a thousand times before it occurred to me I could do anything about it. I generally wait for someone else to make it clear what I should be doing or what should be done. I feel no agency over objects or buildings or infrastructure. The county comes and rights the downed sign the very next day.

After that, a galvanized pipe beneath our kitchen sink gives in to corrosion, our beloved cat Moon goes missing, and a filling from Stan's tooth falls out. Our friend Kristen comes over at 8 am Saturday morning to organize a search party in the midst of dealing with a heartache of her own. Stan is in the fetal position on the floor, convinced the gray tabby he's given his whole heart to is already dead or at least missing forever. *He's a cat,* says Henry.

He'll come home when he's hungry. I hold my own anguish at bay by deciding Moon is on a great adventure, a rite of passage, marking his own transition from boy to man.

It feels good to walk through the neighborhood stapling laminated missing signs to wooden posts, talking about the nature of love and friendship and what can thread itself through a heart to tear apart the two. We talk to neighbors, rattle dry cat food in Tupperware containers, call out in soft, sweet voices to soothe ourselves as much as the still wild, lost animal we are trying to call home.

When Henry and I get back to the house we all eat a big breakfast of eggs and sausage and biscuits Stan made while we were gone. We set out a bowl of warm tuna fish and a litter box and everything else people suggest we do. I call a plumber and Stan calls a dentist. Moon's sister, Sun, never leaves my side, climbing onto my chest and licking my face.

Moon comes home after 36 hours away in the middle of the night, hungry. We feed him and cry with relief. We are learning what it is we are able and not able to do.

Groundhog

Stan and I are spending a weekend at the Downtown Omni. It is glorious though I always relate more to the wait staff, maids, and valets than the other guests. We have an interesting foray down the back stairs that leads to a locked door opened up for us by a janitor, a pieced-together southern alley-man with winged hair and a deep voice. He leads us laughing, first through what seemed to be his quarters and then through many empty cavernous ballrooms, so much inflated space.

We are on the eighth floor with a view of some rooftops and train tracks and glimpses of our familiar brown, snaky James River. The hotel sends us chocolate-covered strawberries and sparkling cider, which we gorge on after gorging on dinner—ridiculously lavish excess that those who are actually wealthy probably avoid.

Between courses, we walk up to the flood-wall and past murals painted last summer and to the pipeline where Stan and Henry go fishing on Sunday mornings. There are clusters of girls crouched down on the hillside drinking cans of beer in high-heels and tank tops and I remember being them—single, carefree, and out on a

Saturday night before getting married a million years ago. And then we see a groundhog scuttling along across our path, fat and cute and happy and I feel just like that groundhog feasting greedily upon the rich green grass of the world.

Ready to Lead

Henry says he feels like a video game character out of weapons and health thrashing around desperately trying to terminate the last few weeks of sixth grade. He has been running a rigorous campaign for treasurer of the SCA.

Stan and I did not have what you would call school spirit but we are trying to support him the best we can. Henry has over a 100 point average in his advanced math class and is playing up the nerd aspect of his candidacy. *I'm the least popular candidate but the most qualified,* he tells me. Last week another sixth-grader came up to him and said, *No one's going to vote for you,* and Henry said back, *If you've heard of me, I'm doing something right.*

I want to go beat up that little asshole, I say to Henry. *Mom, I've handled it,* he says. *That was a comeback I prepared the moment I started my campaign.*

I'm very proud of you, I say. *Still that little asshole better sleep with one eye open.*

In the afternoon we find out that Henry has won his race for Treasurer of the SCA!!! The day is full of celebration, dinner out at his favorite Mexican restaurant, and ice cream in the backyard with close and precious friends, including his award-winning campaign manager, Charlie. The tide turns however at bedtime when Henry starts to think about his running mates, the two boys in the sixth grade he'd run against.

What if I crushed their dreams? he sobs. *I know they tried really hard. What if they really needed this?* His tears are so big I start crying, too. *I knew losing would be hard but I had no idea it would be hard to win,* he sobs and we talk about balance and empathy and how to be a humble public servant rather than a power-hungry tyrant.

In the morning he feels better. *I'm ready to lead now,* he says, his eyes bright and dry.

Supernova

This morning as I walk out to my car, I see that my windshield is no longer there. Or it is there, but it's in shards and splinters, crystals, massive snowflakes, a supernova of glass. The explosion of my windshield is peppered with pumpkin seeds and bright orange pumpkin meat.

Thankfully nobody's been hurt except the pumpkin. I call the police, insurance, auto glass repair, and my sponsor. The cop who comes over asks if we can think of a motive and I say *maybe my Obama stickers? That's reason enough*, he says, turning around laughing, and I mumble *fuck you, buddy, fuck you.*

Stan's friend who is on the way over to demo our kitchen, lets me borrow his truck to come to writing class. The truck bed is full of yesterday's rubble—our chimney, as a matter of fact. Now there's a hole in the roof of our house. You can stand on the refrigerator and look up and see the sky.

Before class, I return a frantic message to an old friend. Carter's apartment caught fire last night and he is at MCV in critical care from smoke inhalation. Carter Graham. My first boyfriend.

If you are estranged do you show up in the hospital room asking forgiveness? Giving forgiveness? Or do you say a silent prayer and hope to god, god hears you? When the burns are bad do you forget your own thin skin, make amends, make peace, makeup at all costs? Or do you let what was said and done be buried with the bones?

When the man in the burn unit has the word love tattooed on his arm in your handwriting do you demand to see under the covers, what's left, what was singed, what remains? Who gets cremated and who lives on in this new skin? Who did you show up for when you could? Who knows how much you loved them?

Survival Mode

Stan goes to Home Depot to buy a dishwasher and a sink for our gutted kitchen but forgets to buy the sink. And now we've run out of money. I spend the day talking myself into being a frontier woman, a pioneer. Hell, I used to go camping all the time! My friend Neala lives in a yurt. She doesn't even have a sink to forget to buy.

I eat french fries and mayonnaise for dinner, microwave my husband a meatball Hot Pocket, and my son some frozen chicken nuggets, all of which seem like a superhuman cooking achievement because there are loose cabinets and sheets of drywall fencing in all the necessary appliances. I never can reach the ketchup. In the midst of it all, a friend leaves a long voicemail on my cell phone ranting against the evils of microwaves, pleading with me to use a crockpot instead, insisting it doesn't have to come to this. Oh, but it does. We're in survival mode. We will do what we have to do to survive.

I talk myself into a calm and steady NPR state of mind even though it's not really the sink I'm thinking about. It's the death, all the death, and we all know that when your friends die and there's no place to wash your hands you are liable to lose it just a little. My friend and student Timothy died in a motorcycle crash a week after Carter died from the fire and there are memorials being held for each of them a week apart in the same renovated warehouse downtown. My heart is tender and raw and confused and broken. There's something about desperately needing the rest of the world to work properly when everything else is falling apart and exploding and crashing and catching on fire and smashing all around.

But then Stan comes home with hot food and says that the woman he's installing a new TV for is going to give us her granite countertops and sink, one that will fit perfectly into our new cabinets.

The man I hate this morning, I love at night, and the only thing that changed was me.

Distant Kingdoms

Stan goes back to Home Depot and returns with all of the framing and plywood necessary to turn the front porch into an office. We have just learned, based on our credit score, that we will not be moving anytime soon. We spend 10 hours working hard as hell, sweating, and hammering and I remember that I actually do love working with him when we are able to work together at all.

We fall in bed barely able to move, our joints 8000 years old. The next morning the old fear sets in. Will he finish this project or abandon it halfway through? Could this new room be the answer we've been desperately seeking or just more unfinished space where we can tear each other apart?

In my dream, Stan takes down all of the work he's done to the porch addition and I scream and cry and keen like someone is killing me.

This Animal

When I get home from a morning of teaching, I strip off my bra and earrings, take my hair down and climb straight into bed. A cat climbs on top of me and a dog stretches out along my length. Henry comes in to do his homework. I fetch us snacks and after we eat I stare at the ceiling tossing, turning, trying to wind down from the wild excitement my mind has been generating. When Stan comes home he climbs into bed with the rest of us. At some point, I crawl out to make dinner.

I feel like a feral animal, I say.

You look like one, he says.

I wonder what other people do during these middle hours of the day? Something productive? I can't imagine. I have to shut everything out for a few hours before I can take it all in again. I've been trying to practice self-care for the last couple of years. Once I prided myself on being low maintenance, not needing anything, not even a shower. Now I need yoga, meditation, 12 steps, 57 vitamins, yoga, meditation, and prayer just to get out of bed. I've had to step up my game because life has stepped up her game, too.

Do you want to grow, to expand? life asks. *You better take care of yourself, girl.* Yesterday I did take care of myself. I took care of myself by eating four mini chocolate croissants standing up at the kitchen counter. Sometimes I take care of myself by asking for help, sometimes by giving it.

I show up to talk to other people who need help at least once every day, my sponsees, students, child. It makes me feel less crazy, less alone. I stop and take a bath when I need to, I walk every morning so I can see the growth of bamboo by the creek on East Valley Road. It takes a lot to take care of this animal with changing needs and moods both rough and tender. I'm doing it the best I can.

The other day I lay down for a 10-minute meditation and took a 2-hour nap. When I woke up my husband was cleaning the shit out of our living room that doubles as his storage shed. It actually glistened. He'd swept enormous piles of dog hair into the trash and found a bin for everything. I decided to clean, too. I took the gorgeous, dead Mother's Day roses from the dining room table and threw them out the back door, but instead of complying, the rose petals scattered in arcs around me on the floor halfway between outside and in, where they were meant to go and where they weren't. Instead of sweeping them up, I took a picture and then left them there. They were beautiful just as they were.

Breath of Fire

When I enter yoga I instinctively move as far away from the handsome bearded man as possible, finding myself unfortunately positioned in front of the big mirrors, facing the rest of the class instead. *Calm down,* I remind myself. *This is for you.* And I unroll my mat, desperate to connect my mind with my body. These days desperate can also mean uncomfortable. I am the Princess and the Pea. Small splinters are great arrows.

The focus of the class is breathing which I have noticed in other yoga classes lately I don't know how to do. I often find myself gasping—not because I'm winded but because the air has displaced itself and I have to chase after it, gulp it down before it disappears.

The yoga instructor leads us through Breath of Fire, Breath of Joy, deep stomach breaths, nose breaths, breaths where we look and feel like wild animals caged up in the same room. I am grateful for the opportunity to practice because it all feels pretty important. We move, too. I stretch and roll and reach and bend, telling myself I am re-entering my body, that it is a safe and OK place to be.

I only make the mortal error of looking in the big mirror once and then gently force myself to be kind to the girl staring back. Everyone else is just there with me, not worse or better. I am not on display, I am practicing introducing my mind to my body like everyone else.

The instructor apologizes for a short savasana but I think all the breathing brings it home fast. *You were not a mistake,* I hear from somewhere deep inside as soon as I close my eyes. Hot tears spill over and I can see and feel and hear the little girl whose parents loved her but could not figure out how to love each other. The little girl who carried this feeling without words to frame it: if my mother and father's marriage wasn't meant to be what of anything that came out of it?

I don't have to force myself to be kind to the girl who asks these questions. My love for her comes hot and steady, like breath.

The Dance

I know it is time to go to a dance class the morning after I attend a Native American sweat lodge ceremony in the woods. I've had an ongoing war with my body and I'm tired of the fight. I want to try something different, something that scares the shit out of me, something I know will change me for the good.

The dance class is held in a spacious warehouse with wooden floors, a ballet barre, and a wall of mirrors in Scott's Addition. There are no rules or steps or directions for the dance. We are just told to listen to our bodies and let the music guide our hands, our elbows, our necks, our feet.

The other dancers are every shape and size, doing their own thing, and thankfully, not paying attention to me at all. I start on the floor, curled up in a ball. As the tempo increases, I begin, slowly, to move. And then I'm whirling and twirling and jumping, and at times nearly running around the floor.

The music pushes me, pulls me, holds me, and then throws me further across the room. I dance so hard, sweat pours down my forehead and thighs. At the end, I collapse exhausted and happy and swollen with a new feeling of life coursing through my blood. I can't stop smiling. I go back the next Sunday and the next, and every Sunday morning I possibly can.

Brilliant and Brutal

I meet Tim in my Tuesday night creative nonfiction writing class. He is one of the students with whom I feel an instant connection. His writing is so visceral and provocative I sense I'm in the midst of literary greatness when he reads his work out loud. He also feels familiar, like somebody I've known for lifetimes, or at least since high school.

Like my dad, he is a woodworker with an expansive imagination. His writing about his relationship with music and his persistent mental illness is brutal and brilliant. After a couple of workshops we figure out that we must have known each other after all—he dated one of my close friends in college.

Yes, he agrees. *We're from the same tribe.* When he tells me he wants to continue with classes but can't afford it, we agree on a barter. He begins to help out around the writing studio, fixing jammed locks, taking out the trash, building bookshelves, running errands. When we move out of the upstairs of Chop Suey into a building down the street where we can grow and expand, he helps us pack.

In addition to odd jobs, because Tim reads my stories and edits manuscripts for our new small press, he comes to be known as the King and the Janitor of Life in Ten Minutes. Eventually, he helps at my house as well, repairing trim and broken floorboards and various unfinished projects we can't seem to tackle. When he starts staying for dinner, he becomes friends with Henry and Stan, too.

I'm surprised and happy to become close to a man with whom I can talk about feelings *and* writing. I am able to share deeply and vulnerably with him about my relationships, my struggle with co-dependency, and my writing process. He has strongly defined boundaries and our friendship forms slowly, and with great clarity. He says we are each other's training wheels, learning how to have a friendship that doesn't veer us precariously off the track of our separate, but intertwined lives.

Wilderness

I am at a writing retreat in the mountains. I have notebooks—new and old. Pens—black and blue. Coffee and a spectacular view of the countryside overlooking a perfectly inviting wooden desk. There are three other writers here—dedicated, beautiful, serious writers providing the perfect backdrop and setting for creative explosion. Only there doesn't seem to be a single thing inside of me ready or willing to explode.

I look at the thicket of forest outside my window on the other side of the gently moving blanket of fog and feel like I've been dropped off in the wilderness by helicopter with only a machete. No GPS, no compass, no guide.

I have traveled here before, cutting swaths of path through impenetrable forest blow by blow. I just didn't expect to find myself here again. Or if I did I thought I'd know how to get out and where to go.

Helen and I take a steep, hot walk through the mountains. The sun blazes while raindrops the size of wet plums pelt us at intervals.

Covered in sweat and with blistered feet from my poor choice of shoes, we cut through an opening in the trees to find the river where we wade before surrendering our bodies, fully clothed, to the delicious cold of the water.

At night we sit on the cushioned rocking chairs of the front porch as lightning flashes across the night sky in a fantastic display of fireworks and thunder. God is really showing off in pure and vibrant grandiosity, as strings of white Christmas lights twinkle like fireflies along the railing.

The river and the storm are pure heaven but they do not tell me what kind of book I need to write next or what direction to set out from in this place of not knowing. This doesn't mean I can dig a hole to bury myself in or that I should light SOS flares for rescue. Just that I'll have to set out eventually, making up the next route, trusting I will figure it out, that it will emerge, as I go along.

One Connection

I receive an email this week from a woman who was at my last race writing workshop. She tells me that she had to read the *Halfway House for Writers* slowly so she could digest its full impact, that it's the closest she's come to reading her own thoughts and feelings before, that it gave her permission to be not just a writer, but a human being.

This email saves my spirit after a gut punch rejection this week from the agent Jeannette Walls referred me to when I met her years ago. *It's clear you're talented and I like your style but the market is terrible for memoir right now. I don't think I could sell it to a publisher.*

All I can hear is *I can't get behind this book enough to take the risk.* My sponsor tells me her Baptist pastor preaches that *rejection is God's redirection.* My redirection has been turning my back on the viper pit of hideous thoughts trying so hard to find tender flesh. I knew you weren't good enough, who do you think you are? What do you think you're trying to do?

I've been in a dark room with my writing opening doors trying to find a light in the hall. I have to trust that my book will be delivered into the right hands whether it's one pair or a few or many. The email I received this week was a feast for the ages, a reminder that one connection can help keep me fed.

Unzipped

I am asked to guest teach a workshop for a feminist ethnographies class at VCU. There are trans men and trans women, black gay men and straight white women, hes, shes and theys. Everyone writes deeply, gut-level deeply, honestly vulnerable about their experience on the outside of cultural norms, their layers of existence, memory, identity, self, fitting in, standing out, separation, grief, how to find oneself in the face of an outsider identity.

Their themes are transition, racism, ageism, sexism, how to find and feel at home when you're an army brat and a black woman constantly on the move, how to identify as a woman when your beard has grown in, how to study racism when you're white, how to look at gender when you're trans, how to reconcile your childhood with a self that has suddenly become old.

There are tears and laughter and ahas and big sighs and a meeting of our hearts around the table. I do not feel like an outsider coming in, but one of the tribe they've never met, how it feels in every room when we unzip our gendered colored aged skin and let our insides hang out all bloody and pulsing and beautiful together.

I Choose Me

I want to be chosen, I tell my therapist.

Then you need to choose yourself, she tells me.

Uggghhhhh.....nnnnooooooo....guggggghhhh, I wail. *I don't want to choose myself! I want everyone else to!* I have done so much work. On my defects of character, on my chakras, on my god-shaped-hole. I know better. I just don't always feel better.

Somewhere along the way, I ingested the terrible belief that I am only as worthy as I am wanted. And the cruel catch is that I have to want to be wanted by someone who could never, ever truly want me back. In fact all my life I've had the uncanny ability to choose the person in the room most incapable of love to be the wellspring of my self-esteem. The difference now is that as soon as I see that person, I run.

Reversing this deeply ingrained, terribly misguided malfunction of my DNA has taken everything I have. Affirmations, meditations, therapy. The good news is I'm not alone. When Sarah comes over she tells me she is going on a diet. I look at her in horror. *Not that kind of diet,* she says. *A diet from needing outside approval from anyone other than myself.*

Ah yes, the best-worst kind, I agree. I have come so far. I still have so far to go. I no longer allow people in my life who make me feel like shit. I don't try to convince anyone that they should have loved me more. The dance class I'm taking is all about my relationship with my body, mind, and soul and it is glorious. I have found that when I look in the mirror I see someone I would choose to have as my own partner every single day of the week. But I still can't post a photo of myself I find unflattering. I still notice how I'm noticed and how I'm not. I want to say that this year I Choose Me. But it's not a one-time choice. It's a choice I'll have to make again and again until there's only myself to choose.

Golden Shadow

I'm reading a book about our shadow side. So many human beings refuse to believe we have the capacity to be evil, predatory, greedy, and vicious. Doing shadow work requires us to claim all of the unclaimed parts of ourselves. But some of us have lived most of our lives in the negative polarities already. We don't need anyone to tell us we have the ability to be bad, worthless, ugly, stupid or selfish. We know all too well. And that's where the Golden Shadow lies. The beautiful and brilliant parts of ourselves we have long denied. The Golden Shadow. These words ring in my head for days. What's in my Golden Shadow?

By Sunday morning at dance class, I know. *Wanted.* I am wanted. It is a volcanic explosion. Unwanted, rejected, cast aside, and unchosen, those feelings have chased me my whole life.

Starting with my dad who dropped me off at my mom's, going back home thousands of times without me. A fear of abandonment that has infiltrated friendships, marriage, men. Choosing men who want me, then don't, on and off, and on and off again. But I realize I *am* wanted. I am. It is like a steroid to poison ivy. Calm and peace settling around my skin.

The House is My Manuscript

This week, while dragging debris and cutting brush and cutting siding and measuring fence posts I realized this month is the very first month without any sort of manuscript to edit or continue or slog through in a very, *very* long time.

My memoir is in the hands of a third agent. The anthology, a collection of creative nonfiction pieces written by my students, is ready to launch. And because it is the first time in a bazillion years I'm not writing, editing, or gnashing my teeth overwriting, I have turned my focus towards my greatest source of pain since becoming a homeowner: our house. It is so hard to care for something you never really wanted! I always wanted a 33rd-floor apartment or a haunted farmhouse or to travel my whole life without any keys or address so while buying the house I grew up in was both a necessity and in many ways a blessing, it wasn't exactly a dream come true.

After years of wanting someone else to take over, my house is my manuscript now. One I am at last co-writing instead of demanding someone else author for me. While my husband has knocked out walls, laid new floors, installed new windows, and spent God knows how much time in the crawl space doing God knows what, I've never seen work on the house as my responsibility. And that has been miserable for both of us.

But something has been changing inside of me. I have become willing to actively participate in this aspect of my own life.

And so, my husband and I spend all three days of Memorial Day weekend building a fence, hauling lumber, and hanging siding—my own requisite blood, sweat, and tears shed. The entire emotional gamut visited. But it isn't the cursing that surprises me. It's the bliss. My husband is so happy I finally care about our house, it's as if he married another woman. Sweating, lifting, hauling, and heaving all weekend feels like the physical manifestation of a long-overdue remodel of, not only our house but our marriage.

As I cut the siding and he nails it onto the back of our house, I feel like this is somewhere I could live and he is someone I can live with. I never wanted to get dirty working on my house before and now that's all I want.

Small Kingdom

I had to learn how to love and appreciate and be grateful for my house before I was able to leave it. And now it's finally happening. We are moving. After 19 years of living here, our house goes on the market tomorrow and the photographer comes to take pictures this afternoon. Our house looks like it's inhabited by strangers. Clean strangers with strange taste.

And now we are about to buy what to me, feels like a small kingdom. I swooned the moment I stepped into the old empty 1968 house— last updated in 1983—with three fireplaces and a 70s hot tub and a two-car garage and a yard and a treehouse and a sunroom with skylights and so many big, light-filled rooms, I could barely stand it.

It had been empty almost a year and when we showed interest the selling agent started courting us religiously. Our real estate agent said the house was super janky but it was still over our price bracket. We kept looking but nowhere else took my breath away like this house did.

Last Friday we made an outrageously low offer but one in our price range. After a couple of negotiations, our offer was accepted. My heart thumps fast when I think about it. It feels like Christmas morning except Christmas is still four weeks and five days away. We'd love to move up the closing date, we're so ready to be able to let go and spread out, to unfurl and breathe. This is not just a house, this is not just a move, it's the completion of one massive round of karma and the beginning of another.

His Next Wife

This morning before the sun comes up, Stan and I sit in our new sunroom and share gratitude lists with each other. We don't usually do this sort of thing, we usually save sweet, deep meaningful stuff for therapists and sponsors but neither of us has been to a meeting for a week so I thought it couldn't hurt. *I'm so grateful for our health,* I said, *and that we're not still crammed together in our old house.*

I'm grateful for my first wife, Stan says and then I hit him with a pillow. *Your last wife,* I correct. *If I did get married again,* Stan says, *I'd need you to set it up for me.*

OK, I say. *I've got the perfect woman picked out for you. Her name is Helga and she has the face of a potato!*

She has a hairy elbow, Stan chimes in. *And a uni-boob* I say. *That she wears in a tube top.*

She wears socks with Birkenstocks, Stan says and we continue to create his next wife until I am in tears of laughter.

My White Neighborhood

In the middle of the week my son and I create and install his idea for a 57-foot-long, 5-foot-tall *End Police Brutality* rainbow art installation in the front yard of our very white, very suburban neighborhood. As we work, a small blonde girl with pigtails rides slowly by on her pink bike scrutinizing each name.

They don't even have George Floyd! I hear her whisper to her friend. *Yes, we do!* I yell from across the lawn. *We're just not finished yet!* Some neighbors come out of their houses to look or to ask questions. Other neighbors walk right past us, their faces pointing straight ahead as if they can see nothing at all.

The mail carrier and the UPS driver, both African-American men, pull over at the same time, park, and get out of their trucks. We stand around taking pictures, telling stories, smiling, laughing, and nearly crying through a moment of profound connection. If there wasn't a pandemic, I'm pretty sure we would hug, too.

While we are watching TV, the doorbell rings. A woman who'd grown up in our house stands in our yard with daughters of her own. Her father died this morning, just weeks after her mother, she tells us. We bought this house from them exactly a year ago, in June. We have mutual friends, she tells me. And one of them shared a photo of Henry's art installation on Facebook that afternoon. *I had to come see it,* she says, with tears in her eyes. *I've never seen the house look so good.* I cry, too. In so many ways this is my dream house, and I love our city. But it has been white-washed with the insidious disease of racism for centuries too long.

The next night we go to the *Black Lives Matter + Justice for George* protest that begins at Monroe Park and marches to the 4th Police Precinct on Chamberlayne Avenue. The people are every age and color of skin. The chants are passionate and the feeling is energized and fierce. I have never seen my city look so good.

Peace and Joy Hunted Me Down

One cat curls into my lap and one cat curls into Stan's as we sit in front of the fire and it is like I've reached late-stage nirvanic bliss. I see a male and a female cardinal perched on either side of our bird-feeder and it feels like I've won a large cash prize. I make a potato leek soup recipe from scratch and an apple crisp from the apples we picked at the orchard. My dad meets a man he can have a conversation with at memory care. *He reminded me of my father and therefore myself,* my dad said and my heart is full. We go to see my mom in a beginner's improv performance and it is as if she were making her Broadway debut. The neighbors have a new baby cow who is red and beautiful and comes so close to my outstretched hand I can see her pink wet nose and I want to scream *YES YES YES* and before she reaches my hand she throws her body around and head butts the other baby cow and my life is basically complete.

I know balance is temporary. That life is so fucking fragile, that we're all teetering on the edge of a pin and can be pushed off at any moment by death or illness or accident or tragedy or upheaval but for now, we are in orbit, and we spin.

Wherever He Needs to Go

Henry and I have been taking long walks together, sometimes multiple times a day. I'm his sounding board, brainstorm buddy, ethics guinea pig, and philosophy experiment. I listen and respond as best I can with true interest. I'm now speaking back to an actual human being with a functioning processing system. And while he has less life experience he has a mind more open and hungry and ravenous for learning and ideas and questions and knowledge than ever before.

I worry because I'm not his teacher or mentor or friend or peer. Those all effectively vanished in the last 53 days since the pandemic began and I know I can't fill those roles but neither can I disappear completely into my own world. I am determined to stay as present and available as possible to him. In the last month, he has read *Notes from Underground*, *Crime and Punishment*, a 500-page history of philosophy book, a book called *Science and Religion*, *The Bell Jar*, and *Astrophysics for People in a Hurry*.

He wonders if he should be a diplomat or a journalist or professor, sociologist or senator or environmental lawyer. I just hope I can keep up enough and help him get wherever he needs to go.

Rosh Hashanah

My mother asks me to pick up sour cream, candlesticks, and—if I have time—to select a couple of prayers for Rosh Hashanah dinner at her house tonight.

I spend the afternoon on the internet looking at pictures of men blowing shofars, apples dipped in honey, and page after page of suggestions for how to hold your own home ritual, high holy-day style.

I select several official-looking prayers, two poems by the poet Marge Piercy, the astrological significance of Rosh Hashanah as it falls on the first day of the month of Libra, a Kabbalistic interpretation of the New Year, some really bad jokes about rabbis, illustrated memes like *Shofar, so good,* and directions for how to recite the Tashlich, preferably by a river with fish, but whatever you do DON'T FEED THE FISH.

I print out three copies of this DIY handbook and bring them to my mother's house along with the candlesticks and sour cream, feeling more at home in the role of Jewish daughter than perhaps ever before.

My mother's table is glorious with a colorful table cloth, apples, and honey, slivers of almonds, a bowl of fresh figs, chalices of freshly blended raspberry smoothies, the family's silver candlestick holders. I've never led the prayer before but last night we read and laughed and listened and ate every morsel of brisket and apple cake.

I want to be inscribed again in the Book of Life, as much or more than I've ever wanted it before.

A New Season of Marriage

I'm on a walk with a friend who has been married for two years. She's afraid because she no longer feels in love with her husband. She's afraid her marriage is falling apart.

Oh God, if marriage was about feeling in love all the time, marriage would be obsolete, I tell her. This used to crush me. Like solidly point-blank fucking crush me. I could never fall in love with someone else, ever again? It felt like preparing for a long and painful death.

Stan and I are in a new season of marriage. They say that wherever you go, there you are, that geographic cures don't work, and that you take your problems with you, but I think in this case we are the exception to the rule.

In our new house, we don't fight over space, territory, possession, who gets to put what, where. He doesn't feel like a visitor in my house and I don't feel haunted by the ghosts of my parents. Maybe it's Al-Anon and the meds and the therapy, but personally, I think it's probably the house.

I no longer cringe when I get home and see his truck in the driveway. I don't long for one of us to go out of town without the other. I don't fantasize about my own apartment or his accidental death.

Have you fallen back in love with Stan? my friend asks.

No, and yes, I say. *It's not like the first time falling in love. That was vertical. This is horizontal. It's love widening.*

Free

We moved about seven months ago now and at least a couple of nights a week I dream that we didn't. I dream we are still at our old house which is inevitably in a state of extreme chaos and disrepair. I dream that our real estate agent forgot about us and we've been frozen in limbo mid-move. I dream we did move but the deal fell through and we have to move out and back into our old house. Sometimes there are black eels and murders in the neighborhood.

Every single time I wake up I am so relieved to discover it was just a dream. We did move. We are out. We are safe. We are in the new house, *our* new house and there's no one making us move out. I told Stan about yet another oh-my-god-we-didn't-move nightmare and he said I guess it makes sense—you spent your whole life there. And though it's where I got sober and married and had a child and found myself as a writer and a woman and tried to practice gratitude as much as I could, I felt like my childhood home was a web I was trapped in.

Book 3

A Brief and Fantastic Celebration of Life

And it's such a sad old feeling
All the fields are soft and green
It's memories that I'm stealing
But you're innocent when you dream

— Tom Waits, *Innocent When You Dream*

Crow

My dad had a pet crow when he was a boy growing up in the Blue Ridge Mountains of Shenandoah. He bought the crow from another little boy in his class who'd been throwing rocks at the crow's mother. A smoker by the age of 8, my dad taught Seymour how to smoke cigarettes, too. Seymour perched on my dad's shoulder while he played baseball, running the bases like lightning in the wind.

My dad was heartbroken when after almost a year together, Seymour flew away. A murder of crows called to him from the trees and Seymour flew up to join them, never returning to my dad again.

Mobius Strip

Before I was born, my Dad was a social worker in the forensics ward of a psychiatric hospital. Reality has doubled back on itself and gotten stuck in a logic loop and now he's the one in the institution and now he is the one we call insane. One of his patients used to quote T.S. Eliot by heart and now my dad quotes it to me, and as I drive him from the memory care center to our house I experience a sense of déjà vu for a life that wasn't even mine. Maybe the way a little girl who was hopelessly in love with her father faces reality is by caring for him as his mind and body crumble, like elaborate sand sculptures swept into the sea.

I grow old ... I grow old ...
I shall wear the bottoms of my trousers rolled.

Shall I part my hair behind? Do I dare to eat a peach?
I shall wear white flannel trousers, and walk upon the beach.
I have heard the mermaids singing, each to each.

I do not think that they will sing to me.

— T.S. Eliot

Maybe it's just the pattern God created—we help those die who helped us live—we usher each other in and out of this world on the mobius strip of life.

Visions

My dad lives on a lake with a couple of acres and keeps track of the geese and the beavers, the moles, voles, fish, cranes, and many birds of prey. He names them and talks to them and tells me he would rather die than be moved into the city or worse, the assisted living facility the doctors say he'll need if he becomes too sick.

He talks to the animals and a spectrum of ghosts and haunts, some living, some dead. Civil War soldiers, rednecks, Mexican immigrants, and his own mother—Grandma Billie—appear to him to tell him things. Dinosaurs chase alongside the riding lawn mower as he drives and small creatures of every description fly by his feet as he walks. Sometimes Henry and I are there too, and he tells us things but we vanish before we can say anything back.

My father has had visions his whole life, has been called a shaman, a medicine man, and a master carpenter, but I love thinking of him as the little boy with the crow best.

Falling

In the grocery store, my son starts flailing his arm wildly, all around. *Like Papa,* he tells me. *I'm doing this because Papa does it,* and I tell him, *Papa can't help it, it's part of his disease,* and Henry says, *Well, it feels good, I like it,* and I wonder how much of my dad my nine-year-old will know apart from the hallucinations and other worlds of Lewy Body Dementia with Parkinson's. It's a disease unlike any other, wrapped so thoroughly through mind-body-spirit.

On a recent visit my dad's back went out and he had to crawl up the stairs screaming out in agony every few minutes. I stood helplessly and wept, hiding my face while Stan made sure he didn't fall back and Henry cheered, *Go, Papa, go! You can do it!*

It's a blessing and a curse to know what I do, to have loved this man to a fault when he was only sometimes there for me. To watch him fall.

The Brain Anchor

It's not until I'm on I-95, driving to visit my dad, that I realize what to do with the fur hat tied by ropes to a cinder block in the trunk of my car—a brain anchor used as a prop by a friend in a surrealism creative writing class. My father not only introduced me to the world of surrealism when I was a child, he currently inhabits it.

I'd called him the day before to ask his permission to write about him because—I tell him— there's nothing else right now I can imagine writing about. Still, I feel like a vulture scavenging for blood. *Oh, of course you can,* he says, surprising me as he always does with his generosity. *I would be honored.* And then he suggests I write an even longer article for a national magazine because people love to read about other people's dying parents.

But, Dad! I say horrified. *You're not dying!*

I've had another home invasion, Valley, he tells me. *It's time to stop driving. I'm deteriorating.*

What kind of home invasion? I ask, but I already know. After suffering a series of micro strokes two years ago, a string of MRIs and psychiatric evaluations turned up the words inconclusive, abnormal, psychosis, hallucinations, and dementia.

Perhaps I'm biased, but I prefer my dad's definition of his shifting mental state to anything I've found online. He described his first extended hallucination as *a cosmic, horrific supernatural freak show of Southern holiness.* A tall man with lobster claws for hands and his very short 300 lb wife—who together looked like a period and an exclamation point—were the leaders of the pack. *They were hungry and fat and wanted peanut butter sandwiches,* he tells me. *I thought I was going to be killed, maybe eaten.*

Between trying to beat them away with pillows and making them peanut butter sandwiches, my father called my stepmother and begged her to call the sheriff. She'd assured him it wasn't real and asked him to hang on until she got home. *I know they're hallucinations,* he tells me. *But the real question is, are they still there when I'm gone?*

When I sob to Sarah on the phone, the gravity of the situation finally hitting home, she says, *It's like watching a redwood fall in the forest.* And she's right. My dad has always been fit and tall and handsome but I think it's the largesse of his imagination she's referring to. Growing up, he always kept an open house and an open mind regarding the lines between reality, dreams, poetry, fiction and fact. When I was a child, he opened up the world of story for me. But, at 63, his mind is retreating deeper into the forest.

The characters that populate his imagination have started visiting his waking life. Civil War soldiers ride up to him on horseback; furry white animals streak the yard; pterodactyls soar through the house.

But it's the confusion, the memory loss, the fat illiterate family of rednecks, and the home invaders with whom he's had to make his peace. *I'm much more welcoming to them now,* he tells me. *Which makes them go away faster. The lesson here is that no evil can stand up to humor!*

When I pull into my dad's driveway he's bright-eyed, holding a riotous fistful of purple irises from his garden. I drive him around to do the things he can no longer do by himself and when we're done, I pull the brain anchor out of my trunk. *It's perfect!* he says and shows me a sculpture in the front yard made of bits of metal and discarded scraps of wood.

I call it **stacking,** he says. His new sculptures take on different shapes and unexpected dimensions, becoming more bizarre and more beautiful each day.

Aggressive Self-Care

I go to the massage therapist because there's that thing in my back that appears again and again like a reincarnated demon. I've tried rolling on tennis balls. I've asked my husband to dig his elbow into it. But it hangs on between my neck and shoulder squeezing like a vice.

That's grief, my sponsor says. I've recently been assigned the role of executor over my dad and stepmother's wills. There's no known timeline—it's just an eventuality. The only thing we know is that sooner or later death is coming. And the grief that comes in stages does not wait for death in order to begin.

I've written some really raw, painful things about my childhood recently and sent them to my dad, conversations I'd only tiptoed around before but now feel the need to face head-on. Opening this line of communication has been terrifying but I don't want there to be things unsaid, issues unresolved as we make our way forward. And so, our relationship grows closer, more tender, more painful, more real. It hurts and it heals.

My massage therapist digs her thumbs into my shoulders as I lie on her table. I'm proud just to be there, to have taken the time to practice this level of aggressive self-care. Because in addition to the revolutions in my inner life, my outer life is going full throttle with no end in sight. Workshops, seminars, conferences, birthday parties, mothering, wifeing, housing, adulting, cleaning up cat poop, dog poop, lizard poop, wrestling with the plastic, bloody skeletons of Halloween. Sometimes it feels like I'm running a marathon through a jungle. Even when it's good, sometimes it's just too much. Because now if I crumble and fall, there's so much more to lose.

So. Naps and baths. Forced and prolonged kitten/hound/lizard cuddling. Medication. Meetings. Dancing like a fool. Putting on lipstick to go to CVS. Buying the cute socks. Telling myself I love myself even when I eat the damn cake. Strong, *strong* coffee. Saying no. Going to bed at 6:30. Wearing high heels around the house and comfortable shoes everywhere else. Dancing like a fool. Praying like hell. God, *please.*

This is control, Jodi, my massage therapist says as she rolls her thumbs down my spine, unhooking knots. And it's that too, the deep, desperate need to order the universe so it doesn't spin out. So I don't lose myself and go under. I breathe out heavily under her tender, firm touch and imagine the grief and control losing their grip on my body. As she instructs, I imagine columns of luminescent white light streaming through my power center. I imagine what it would be like if I knew I was OK even awash in the tornadoes and hurricanes and tidal waves of feeling that make up a life. My life. And when she is done, I get up, put my clothes on and dive back into my day.

Angels

This morning I leave the house at 6:30 am and drive through traffic, accidents, and rain on I-95 to pick up my dad and stepmother and drive them to town for her chemo treatment. When Mary was diagnosed with Stage 4 ovarian cancer last year, we were all in complete shock. She was supposed to be the healthy one, the one who would take care of everything and live forever. When I arrive she has a beautiful feathered sky blue scarf wrapped around her head and white linen pants. She's always been able to wear white without spilling food or coffee everywhere like I do. This is further evidence that she's probably an angel.

Despite the traffic and the rain, we make it to the hospital on time and I watch as the nurses insert tubes into her ports, ask questions, read numbers, prepare for takeoff into this part of the day—her third chemo treatment. The cancer has moved into her stomach and her lungs.

Afterward I take my dad to Aunt Sarah's Pancake House and he tells me that when loading firewood out in the country he feels honored and humbled to work in the presence of honeybees.

I think they might both be angels. They've suffered and caused suffering but now they treat every single inexplicable moment of the day like it's a gift from God.

Adult Woman

Driving home after class, my mind flips through my Rolodex of addictions wondering which I can pick to ease the empty feeling clawing at my chest. Miraculously, instead of driving to a bar or Target, I call my sponsor, Billie. She says what she always says. *I know exactly how you feel.* When her parents were battling sickness, dementia, cancer, and death, her abandonment issues were triggered, too.

Until she says it I've had no idea that's what it was. My eyes prick with the sting of recognition.

What have you done in the past when you felt this way? she asks.

Gotten drunk, bought cigarettes or weed, gone home with strange men in bars, I tell her.

She laughs and then pauses. *That's not exactly what I meant,* she says. *What healthy things have you done when you've felt this way?*

Oh, I say. *Cried, written, prayed, made calls, blah blah blah blah. It's just not as fun or as fast though, is it?*

She recommends I go home and listen to a Yoga Nidra in bed under piles of blankets and cats to help create the safety and security of being held in a tight warm hug. When I follow her directions, the tears come in full and so does the complete surrender to the release of sleep. When I get up an hour later I am ready to face the day or at least start cooking.

I bake a spice cake slathered with vanilla icing, two sausage and broccoli quiches, and curry roasted cauliflower to bring out to my dad and Mary's house in the country, wedged into acres of farmland, lakes, and the brightly lit roller coasters and Ferris wheels of the State Fair like a mystical land of country and carnies. My dad moved 15 times before I turned 18 but has lived here ever since. Twenty-five years. It's my home away from home.

After a delicious dinner, the deep pleasure in providing nourishment as a tangible manifestation of love, I take a deep breath and suggest it is time to set a date to talk about their wills. *The ruby-red pitcher that belonged to your Grandma Billie should be yours,* Mary says. I thank her and then with a series of awkward, false starts explain that the division of objects and property is not exactly the conversation I have in mind. Rather, I need to know what happens to one if the other dies. Who wants a DNR? Will it be me making these decisions if the other isn't able? What happens to their bodies when they no longer contain breath?

In two weeks I will return with my laptop to write their answers down. *But how will we get a hard copy if it's on your computer?* my dad asks, technology a distant planet to him now. *Don't worry, I can print it out, Dad,* I assure him, feeling all of those little internal gears and gadgets creating a capable adult woman inside of me begin to snap into place, ready to rise to the occasions that are required of me, heart, mind, body, and soul.

Splinters and Nails

My dad's birthday is tomorrow and I'll bet we're together in not remembering how old he is going to be. Once, he nail-gunned his foot to a roof he was working on downtown and had to be removed by a Medevac helicopter. Once, a splinter sliced through his foot entering from the bottom and emerging through the top. Once, he got a rusty nail in his knee that led to a staph infection and weeks hallucinating in the hospital.

Now some of the worlds he's entered have been the most engaging blends of fact and fiction I've experienced in my life. Before he became a master carpenter, he worked in a mental institution for the criminally insane. He was a social worker at a boys' home in the inner city. The kids called him *The Big-Headed White Man* and he loved that, calls himself *The Big-Headed White Man* still.

He loves living in the country with the beavers and geese and snakes, but sometimes he thinks he's still in the city where he rented apartments like Monopoly pieces, superimposed over the fields and lakes. With his new medications, he tells me his hallucinations are now of the everyday, normal variety and I laugh, jealous. He gave me a suitcase of poetry he wrote before I was born that I open sometimes to decode the mythology, the giant, the wonder of a man I've always found him to be.

Still, I wish his disease were just a splinter to be extracted. I wish it were just a nail we could remove.

How Creative the Body

This weekend I make it up to see my dad. On the screened-in porch, he tells me that he's starting to lose bowel and urinary function, that his eyes are going bad, that he is scared, and that he's not getting better. When I was a child, my dad was all action and mystery. Now that he's ill, he confides in me more. My own busyness becomes knotted and screwed up in my head because how can anything be more important than this?

And then Stan and Henry come in from the lake and say they've seen a turtle belly-up floating near the canoe and when Stan tried to push it towards shore with his paddle, the turtle's guts shot out of its mouth. It smelled *terrible,* they say as my stepmother walks in.

I have some skirts for you, Valley, she says.

Oh, where are they? I ask.

Everywhere, she says.

Everywhere? I ask. *But where did they come from?*

I ordered them on eBay, she says.

Ebay's her new hobby, my dad explains and together they load my arms with jean skirts and leopard print skirts, velvet and floral skirts and skirts encrusted with bells, knee-high and ankle skirts, about fourteen skirts in all, an embarrassment of skirts, and we bundle them into the trunk of my car where they lay in a roll like a dead body.

At home, half the skirts won't pull over the mountain of my hips. It's amazing how creative the body is at inventing new ways to betray us.

Purple Fields of Clover

Mary tells me that my dad is getting better in some ways, worse in others. The men are outside— Stan fishing along the shoreline of the pond, Dad and Henry in the woodshop. *He said he went to the mailbox the other day and as soon as he got back he couldn't remember if he'd gone or not,* she tells me.

But I do that all the time! I say, and I do. We're transferring the chopped-up onions, refried beans, yellow rice, and tofu crumbles into Tupperware containers and I wonder briefly if it's safe for Henry and my dad to be alone in the woodshop together. There are power tools my father still wants to operate but shouldn't.

I know, me too, says Mary, sighing. There are silver streaks in her hair but she's more beautiful to me now than when I was young and her hair was long and black. *Sometimes I'm driving and suddenly I've already arrived,* she says. And then, *let's go find them,* and we walk through the back door to the deck my dad built so I'd have somewhere to stand before walking down the aisle to be married, through the field by their lake.

My dad and Henry are in the shop, holding freshly cut rectangles and circles. *I'm making a car!* says Henry and I think that while they can, we'll let them. I spend the rest of the afternoon walking my new dog Virginia through purple fields of clover that make me catch my breath, zeroing in from millions to one, the delicate flowers we tromp right over.

A Deeply Philosophical Problem

I meet my dad for lunch at a restaurant up the street from my house. He calls to tell me he's on the way but running late. In the end, he arrives right on time. We order fried shrimp Po Boys with lime tartar sauce.

Where were you? I almost called the cops, I laugh. He's always early in contrast to my mother who is always late.

I've had a weird couple of weeks, he tells me. *I feel like Dostoyevsky in* The Idiot.

Well, I feel like Steve Martin in The Jerk, I say back.

There's been another home invasion, he tells me. A home invasion of his own hallucinations, hillbilly rednecks who won't get off his couch, won't stop watching TV. *I just started beating them with pillows,* he says. *Making empty threats because if they refused to move, what could I actually do?*

I put extra french fries in my mouth to muffle the sound of my heart breaking.

I feel I've encountered a deeply philosophical problem, he says. *Only the lesson in it eludes me completely.*

I suggest he tell them to go to the light like he used to tell the ghosts haunting the construction sites where he worked. *Or you could make signs telling them what to do,* I suggest.

I don't think they're literate, he says. *They're more like cats and dogs or disturbed screaming babies. I know they are hallucinations but I wonder if they're still there if I don't see them. I guess it will always be a mystery.*

Here I am, my father's daughter. I always arrive right on time and I'm still inclined to believe all of his stories are true.

The Excrutiating Insignificance
of the Things We Love

When I visit my dad he asks me to come downstairs to see a note he's had Mary write down for him, the palsy in his hands too severe to hold the pen. *The excruciating insignificance of the things we love,* I read and my dad says, *My God doesn't that just grab you by the throat?*

My dad, who said that when I ran away from home at the age of five I shook my fist at *the Gods of Too Littleness.* My dad who gave me Nabokov, Gunther Grass, Charles Bukowski, and Pablo Neruda. My dad, the poet who gave me a beat-up suitcase of his black and white typewriter poems which felt all at once intimate and overwhelming, scorching in their connection to the young man he'd been then and the woman I am now.

Before his diagnosis, but when his hands were already too unsteady to write he asked me to come out to transcribe a collection of thoughts and poems, memories, quotes, and scraps of conversation, the book it seemed to me, he'd always longed to write.

I drove to his house in the country, laptop in hand but when I started putting his pieces together I discovered not remnants of his beatnik poetry, his shamanistic worldview, his deep, rich, and internal world. No. I discovered a pantheon of quotes by Homer Simpson.

If he's so smart, how come he's dead?

Trying is the first step towards failure.

I wish God were alive to see this.

I have yet to make a critical literary analysis of my father's collection, but it still makes us both laugh like crazy.

Dying Warrior

My dad and I have lunch at Ashland Coffee and Tea. We order from the counter, and I add the tip and sign the receipt. His hand shakes too much now to manipulate a pen. I carry our coffees to a window table and the tenderness I feel for this beautiful, kind man nearly breaks me open. He tells me the time on the clock looks like Russian now and after reading a few pages of a magazine or book he starts to read the wrong way, right to left, like Hebrew.

I worshiped my dad when I was little, though so often he was an absence in the spaces his leaving opened up and left behind.

He's vulnerable and open and loving now like a puppy dog or a dying warrior who has no one left to fight, no armor to wear, no more battles to win. We take a selfie with my phone and he says his last selfie was in 1993 when they moved out of the city into the country and transformed an abandoned squatter's house into heaven.

He tells me he worries for my stepmom who is still going crazy on eBay. He says she has four vacuum cleaners and four vita mixes and between her chemo treatments and his dementia I have no idea if these figures exist as fact or fiction. My dad also sees dinosaurs and dead dogs' spirits and ghosts, and he exists now as if two worlds have merged into one.

I Still Have My Dad

Today is one of the strangest visits with my dad yet. When I arrive I say, *How's your day going, dad?* And he says, *Pretty psycho, actually. I've been talking to you all morning. There you are sitting in that chair, there's you over there and then there's the you I'm talking to now.*

And with that, we go to the Y where he says the militant right-winger cornered him with a magazine about escaped convicts and that he nearly fell three times and people were lurching to help him. And then he says, *I really messed up.*

How, dad?

I shampooed my hair with shampoo! Do normal regular people use shampoo to shampoo their hair?

Yes, dad, I say. *And so did you! You did it right!*

Well, hallelujah, he says. *It's a miracle.* And then we go and eat fruit smoothies at the coffee shop.

I saw Tom Rush play a show at this coffee shop, he tells me. *And after the show, he told me how brilliant his son is at opening packages!* Well, I think. This could be true.

When we get back to his house I see he has brought a coffee can full of rocks with him into the car, so we bring it with us into the house along with the rest of his stuff.

I don't feel like crying even when I come in from writing on the side porch to see that he's pulled all the canned goods from the cupboard onto the floor, even when he tells me he has bedbugs, even when my stepmother tells me they're starting to talk about selling the house because right now, today, I still have my dad.

Wild Goose

Tonight we go on another wild goose chase for Virginia at my dad's house in the country. She escapes from the fence in the pasture where my dad and Mary once kept their alpacas. Virginia's joyous run soon eclipses the fence and that's when we start to disperse across the fields like a search party on the hunt for a runaway child. The slippery eel of her sleek body weaves in and out of sight, alluding us.

Calling her name somehow gives her permission to run further afield. Mary, fresh off a particularly nasty round of chemo, gets out of bed to join us in the hunt just as Virginia flops belly down into a rut of deep wet mud and begins to roll in it. We all shout at Mary to go back in the house and get back in bed, but she won't, not until we have Virginia safe in our arms again.

Taking the Wheel

I spent last night with my dad to help him while Mary was away. Before leaving my house for his, I felt sad, tender, and a little afraid. It's so much easier to witness someone's decline from a distance. I hadn't spent the night with my dad in many years and was pre-afraid of feeling too much. The grief I felt, in the end, wasn't for his low moments or his tremor or confusion but for his vitality, the way he could suddenly remember the smell of his third-grade teacher's perfume, an old woman's silver coat jacket button from an Anne Tyler novel, his excitement at our slumber party, his praise for my cooking, the total tenderness in his voice when he talks to Mary on the phone, the way he gets my kid and my kid gets him, his irreverent humor and impeccable attention to detail.

I think I'm doing so well because you and Henry are here with me, he says on the way back from the dump and getting gas for his mower. I'm driving the Ford pickup truck he's had since I can remember— timeless, classic, no before, no after, except now I'm the one who takes the wheel.

Benign Indifference

This morning I wake up in the basement. Mary has decorated the room with dolls which I try not to look at too closely. They moved into this house when I was 17 and I spent my visits home from college getting drunk and high in the basement. Smoking cigarettes and blowing smoke into the fireplace, taking acid and running through the cornfields, skinny-dipping in the lake, driving to the truck stop to drink coffee, and order french fries at 3 AM. Watching the sunrise over the pond through the window over my dad's desk.

I remember what it was like to go to bed at dawn, passing him in the hallway as he was waking up. No reproach, only kindness, only what he refers to as his parenting style of *benign indifference*. My father observed me as if I were a friendly companion sharing his house or his life or his car, approvingly with no strings attached, no rules, no clamping down which made me pry myself from my mother and run as close as I could get without ever completely arriving at him.

Timing

My mother and I are walking Virginia, up and down the hills of our neighborhood, when she says, *I have something to tell you.* My stomach lurches. A lead-in like this never leads to good news. *I haven't wanted to burden you with this,* she continues before a pause. *What is it Mom, I ask. What is it?*

The cancer is back, Valley, she says, and then she apologizes to me that her cancer is back. *Oh my God. Mom. No. I say.*

The timing couldn't be worse, could it? my mother asks. She is so tiny. Her silver hair frames her olive-skinned face and dark eyes. She is my precious little mother and I want to hold her in my arms.

The timing is never good to have cancer, I say. *But yes, now is particularly bad.*

Dad's dementia is rapidly progressing and the cancer in Mary's lungs is too aggressive to deny. Even so, Mary has begun orchestrating their move out of their beautiful, country home and into a rental in the suburbs. All from her hospital bed. She wants

Dad to be closer to us so we won't be left with the task of caring for him and their house when she dies. And she *is* dying.

Everyone wants her to rest but no one can convince her it's a good idea. When dad and I are leaving her room after a visit, she says, *David, don't forget your sunglasses.* Her eyes are closed and her lungs are collapsing, but she sees everything.

Cooking the Latkes

My mother is having surgery for her third cancer recurrence at the University of North Carolina School of Medicine in Chapel Hill this week, and I will drive down and spend a few days with her while she recovers. She is determined to hold the Yane family Hanukkah party this year even if she is bed-bound with a catheter. When she asks me to make the latkes I say, *Mom, I think we might want to hold off on planning just yet.* But she won't hear of it.

There are always too many people, too much food, and a lot of ruckus, banter, hilarity, and insanity at her notorious Hanukkah parties. She wouldn't want it any other way. I used to scrape my knuckles grating the potatoes but now we have a food processor. Even so, the pungent white onions still make me cry.

Make a mountain of white and brown shreds. Heat the oil in the pan until it's hot and squeeze out a handful of the mix with your fist leaving the thick starchy water behind. Don't flip the latkes too soon or they will become mush. Not too late or they will burn. They will take longer to cook than you expect and your cousins and then their children and the boyfriends and girlfriends will be streaming in and out of the front door. Here's a bitchy aunt and a drunk uncle. Here's that cousin with the crude sense of humor who used to answer the phone saying *suck my dick* and the cousin who won't touch the food but brings his own bags of McDonald's instead.

Line up the hot fried latkes on a flat brown paper bag, let the grease seep in. Devour with sour cream and apple sauce like this year might be your last.

Organ Attack

Last night my mother woke up in agonizing pain. She said it's mostly better now and what would the doctors have done anyway, but I hate the idea of her being at home alone while Buddy is away.

I tell her to text me an SOS if she needs something, anything. *I hate to bother you*, she says. I say, *Mom, I have boundaries.*

I assure her that I'm taking excellent care of myself and it's true. Last night I emailed a group of friends and asked if anyone could come over today and help me clean. Sarah Kathleen is coming at 4:30. What kind of miracle is that? This week I found a chiropractor who got to the root of my shooting hip pain. I bought a series of sessions with him at a special monthly rate, throwing in a 10 pack of massage. I'm helping myself so I can help everyone else.

On Sunday afternoon we play Organ Attack with Mom and Buddy. Organ Attack is a card game in which each player starts with five organs that are then attacked over the course of the game by family members using all sorts of nefarious diseases. I give my son cancer. Buddy gives me a stroke. My mom steals my son's nose. I'm not sure if she wins fair and square or if we let her but my mom is the last one of us with any healthy organs left—her tongue. Cancer in my family has wiped away a multitude of sins. Anything hanging on is forgiven. We are all we have left.

The Kind of Woman
I Never Thought I'd Be

My inner gears are shifting into new motion. As I call the realtor to make appointments, as I lead my dad by the hand into the cafeteria, as I pack an overnight bag for Mary and question the night nurse, I feel parts of myself I've never used before standing at attention. The moments when I can function are the moments in between grief when the fog parts.

Yesterday in the elevator on our way to see Mary after her lung collapsed, my dad told me I'm so good at being a grown-up that I should win the Nobel prize. I blushed with pride even though it was only because I was able to find Mary's room after lunch. My Dad and Mary couldn't be more beautiful but they are moving out of their house in the middle of dying and the radio says a hurricane is coming and that is both a fucking horrible disaster and hilariously funny and an opportunity to for me to become the kind of woman I never thought I could be. The one who can show up, make decisions, and get shit done.

Yesterday Tim brought us a homemade cherry pie. Sarah Kathleen brought us a bag of groceries with a label for each item—*crack, blow, heroin, hookers,* and *salad* and I laughed till I cried while happily unwrapping the quiche and banana bread to eat my fill.

For Sale

.

Three days ago my dad and stepmother sold their house out in the country, the house that has been our haven for the last 25 years, the house where my dad finally landed after a life constantly on the move. I immediately hate the people who signed the contract, sight unseen. The *Under Contract* sign is an arrow straight to the gut.

My dad's dementia is exacerbated by stress and his world is a snow globe shaken upside down. This morning their one-eyed cat peed all over the bedroom floor. She refuses to pack. She is staking her claim. She is 19. She is dying. There's no way she will make the move into town.

Today I visit a rental property for my parents. I pay the $40 for the application fee, read the impossible list of requirements we can't get until I have power of attorney—pay stubs, back taxes, credit checks, and signatures. Mary will be recovering from surgery and my dad can't sign his name.

Advanced Human Emotions

Yesterday Henry told me he was going to ask Mr. Brown, the school guidance counselor, to start meeting with him once a week. *I don't want you to be my therapist anymore,* Mom, he said. I felt a pang of rejection and then pride in his self-awareness and ability to ask for what he needs.

He has just written an 18,000-word dystopian short story, applied for the Senate page program, and is writing a TEDxYouth talk. He is a perfectionist and absorbs stress and self-soothes by doing more, just like me. I'm trying to teach him the same lessons that I'm trying to learn myself—that it's OK to *be* rather than *do,* that it's OK to spend time accomplishing nothing, that your self-worth is not your list of accolades.

On Sunday night we walked around the barn, the lake, and the acres of fields on my father's land for the very last time. Henry wept as he remembered details and memories—scavenger hunts, birthday parties, canoe rides, the drawer full of trinkets in the barn that he and Papa shared together. *I wonder if nostalgia and sentimentality are advanced human emotions,* he asked through his tears, *or if humans have always felt them? Cavemen had burial rituals,* he noted a few minutes later. *So, maybe none of this is new.*

Letting All the Love In

This morning I've been hysterically sobbing, calling eldercare lawyers to try to get power of attorney, crawling through the attic looking for lanterns and hurricane gear for the coming storms, arranging to pick up my father to visit Mary after her surgery this morning. I've been on the phone with the landlord of the house my parents are trying to rent and my mother who I yelled at even though she is only trying to help.

I've had moments of great focus and clarity this week and moments of overwhelming grief. The sale of Dad and Mary's house, the loss of my parents as functioning adults, the great unknowns of their future, and the terror of being the one in whose hands big adult decisions will fall.

Right now I need too much and have too little left to give. I've been on the receiving end of homemade pie and dropped-off meals. I'm trying to let all the love in. If I'm functioning at all, that is why.

Big Things

Mary is taken to St. Mary's Hospital by ambulance after her lungs start to collapse again and her neck swells up like a balloon. I decide we are moving Dad into our house. He doesn't want to stay here but it's clear to me he cannot stay on his own. He has started taking the wrong meds, pouring coffee on the floor, and losing his phone.

They've signed the lease on their new house, but yesterday the movers I lined up canceled. They said it was too big a job. *It's too big a job for me too, you fuckers!* I wanted to shout. Last night my dad, husband, son, animals and I huddled together on the living room floor enjoying the welcome distraction of eight tornadoes in the Richmond area. At least these tornadoes were outside the house— and my mind! This morning our cat ate a butterfly and our dog rolled around in something dead behind the shed and I couldn't figure out how to turn on Stan's projector TV that acts as a pacifier for Dad. SOS SOS SOS I texted Stan and he came home from work to turn on the TV. For me the little things are big and the big things are gigantic.

Survival 101

This week my main job is canceling anything and everything extra I have to do. I'm so glad I've had years of experience practicing saying *no, no thank you,* and even *oh, hell no.* No coffee dates, no extra classes, no book reviews, or out-to-dinner dates. Survival 101. Tonight my husband brought home Chicken Fiesta and then my dad did a puppet show with our stuffed Jesus for the bearded dragon and we had a delicious meal and laughed so hard we cried. I felt the rare painful beauty of having my father live in my old childhood bedroom for a week.

He was the absent dad I was in love with and could never possess. I told Tim how weird it felt to care for him and he said the only way to truly heal is to give what you didn't get.

My therapist says it's time to separate the goats from the sheep. Every new task, showering, shaving, dressing, eating a meal, drinking a cup of coffee is a long haul up a steep mountain for my dad. This morning I heard him at 4 AM wandering around the house. He said trying to find a door out of the room was like being locked in Plato's Cave. I set him up with water and a book and tried hopelessly to get back to sleep myself.

Surrender

This morning my father couldn't breathe and we couldn't find the right medicine because he hadn't packed it. The cat brought a chipmunk in who ran wild-eyed and lightning-fast through all of the dark corners of the house. Worst of all, I had to help my dad in the shower.

He was crouched low with the shower curtain wide-open, the nozzle pointed at the ceiling, soap all over his face and eyes. I can't find the washcloth, he said. *This is it,* I thought. *I can't do it anymore. I surrender. Uncle Uncle Uncle.*

We navigated the tricky maze of getting him dried off, dressed, and ready to go, everything from putting on sunglasses, finding Chapstick, and clicking the seatbelt in the car was almost more than we could handle. In the hospital room where I brought him for the morning because I couldn't leave him alone, Mary was doubled over in pain. They put a longer tube in her collapsing lung yesterday.

Mary, I said. *I'm so sorry. I can't handle taking care of Dad anymore.*
I say this to a dying woman, tears spilling hot from my eyes.
My therapist gave me permission and encouraged me to say these
words. Shame and relief flood through me as she said she'll
call her sister. As ashamed as I am, I don't have to do it alone.

Right Here With Me

I contemplate canceling class after my dad breaks down in sobs crying out *I don't know where I am.* I stand next to him and hold one hand on his shoulder while he weeps. I kneel down in front of him, look him in the eye, and say, *You're right here, Dad, you're right here, with me.* He broke down sobbing yesterday too, the grief of so much loss present and impending.

My husband offers to be with him today, thank the lord. Last night Stan borrowed his workbox truck to go get my dad's medical recliner. While moving furniture and sweeping up a year's worth of dust and hair and trash and cords in our tiny house, I find myself cursing, *Jesus Christ Goddamn Motherfucker.*

And then the shame and embarrassment for letting the less than hopeful sweet daughter slips through. My dad's never seen this side of me—my sailor's mouth, my crackling impatience, the boiling over when the pressure cooker gets too hot. I want to suck it back in but I let it hang. There's no way real life can be concealed when you live together for more than a visit on a Sunday afternoon.

Making the Bed

This weekend, when Mary was supposed to get out of the hospital and Dad was supposed to go home, I stripped the beds, washed the sheets, and felt a spaciousness and vitality I don't usually feel. When I learned Mary was staying in the hospital and not getting released, I broke down in sobs and remade the beds. The fact that I have a washing machine and sheets and mattresses is no small matter as I still feel more wild than domestic.

Stan was able to transfer my father's legion of medications and sort them into day and night like a logic problem of moving parts spread across our dining room table. I thanked God for that. Dad sees things that aren't there, rewashes clean dishes, spreads his clothes all over the floor. Last week when he broke down in tears, curled up on our bed like a baby, sobs moving through his body like bolts of lightning, I stood by him, my hand on his shoulder, crying too.

Reversal of Parent and Child

Caring for my father is biblical, unholy. The true reversal of parent and child. This week I've applied ointments to his toes, hand-fed him his meds and food. I have rubbed his back, combed his hair, and helped him pull a T-shirt over his head. I had to buy Preparation H at Target and though of course, I wanted to find it in smooth, suave silence, I ended up yelling, *WHERE ARE THE HEMORRHOID WIPES?* from the middle of the aisle instead.

Yesterday Dad came back from an outing with Buddy in despair about the impending death of their beloved 19-year-old cat. Then, while we had a real estate agent over to our house dad took his clothes and shoes off in the shower and moved all of the blankets and pillows off of Henry's bed onto the floor where I found him taking a nap. He convincingly bamboozled both me and the pharmacist at CVS into believing he no longer needed one of his more important meds which they canceled from the system. And then Dad told my stepbrother we had all ended up in the ER At 3 AM on Mary's deathbed. We hadn't. The patients have left the asylum.

The Gods of Too Littleness

Last night I told my husband I wished my dad and Mary and their cat were all dead. I know being a witness to the end of life is sacred but I'm also exhausted by it and sick of it, too. It's wrenching and terrible and I really want a boring few hours or days. I called my son into our bedroom. *If this ever happens to Dad or me,* I said, *lock us up and shoot us.*

You might regret saying that, he said. But I won't!

I want to write something full of love, wisdom, and acceptance but I'm not there today. I'm angry at them for getting sick, for dying, for leaving us, and for leaving us with so much to do. I am shaking my fist at *the Gods of Too Littleness.*

Just Human

I recently canceled a speaking engagement because I was Just. Too. Overwhelmed. I was torn between guilt and relief until one of the organizers sent me a card: *I am just one Wonder Woman,* read the inside. *Not all of them.* And then my own name. Apparently, this was something I had said when she was a student in my class! Sometimes we have to relearn our own wisdom because we have forgotten it completely. It's still disappointing to not be all the Wonder Women, to have a broken lasso and a downed plane, too. To be more like a child than a superhero. To need to slow down, nurture, play, breathe and heal.

In the last month, I've had to cancel panels, class visits, coffee dates, and even a retreat that for many months I'd been planning to attend. I've decided to quit teaching my night class and I've begun to experience a deeper drawing in. My parents are on a precarious plateau between deep trenches and treacherous valleys. I've had some mental, emotional, and physical health issues of my own to attend to. I've learned that if I'm not deeply centered on the inside I will be a disaster on the out.

It's humbling to not be able to do everything or even most of the things. It's humbling to not be able to save the world or the day, to treat myself as tenderly as I would the child I was.

It's humbling to be human.

HELP

In the last two weeks, I have sobbed, hyperventilated, and lost my shit. I have felt like a toddler having a tantrum and a daughter transforming into a mother. I have cried everything out so I could go on again. I have asked for help and it has arrived like the cavalry.

In the last two weeks, I have helped my father in the shower and held his hand while he sobbed incoherently in a fetal position on the bed. I've toured a facility he said would be nice for other people but that he'd rather die than live in.

In the last two weeks, I've decided one should marry a man solely on the basis of his ability to sort dozens of medications into daytime or nighttime cubes and/or repair medical recliners.

In the last two weeks, I've put on masks and gowns and gloves. I've learned how to drain fluid from a lung and dispose of its contents. I've learned exactly how tenacious, how indefatigable, a woman determined to keep living her life can be.

I have not gone to yoga but I have eaten sour patch kids and brownies in the same sitting. I've accepted gifts of coffee, chicken pot pie, beef stew, country-style donuts, pound cake, BBQ, candles, bath salts, pretend hookers, pretend crack, pretend heroin, pretend blow, real blow-up air mattresses, and bags of salad.

In the last two weeks, I have shared my 980 square foot, one bathroom house with a son, a husband, a father, two cats, a dog, and a lizard. I have redefined personal space and sanity. I have canceled everything not absolutely essential to the immediate act of daily living. I have given help and I have accepted help, too.

It has felt like drowning and then resurfacing, awed by the exquisite and delicious taste of air.

Death and Nursing Homes

Outside of my father's doctor's appointment in the parking lot of Ashland Internal Medicine, my dad practices using the walker my husband bought for him the day before. I pull it from the backseat of my car and then he picks it up and carries it around the parking lot to the curb so he can practice going up and down.

We should go to a nursing home and make a how-to video for old people, he says and everything about the entire scenario is so ridiculous that we laugh and laugh and then fold up the walker and put it in my backseat and I drive us to Walmart.

At Walmart, we pick up a new medication, cat litter, Tylenol, a toilet seat booster, and two tubs of Metamucil, laughing at the insanity of it all, joking about death and nursing homes. We imagine what it would be like to take the Boxing for Parkinson's Patients rehab class. And we buy his dying cat a new bed. Somehow it is fun, the way shopping for coffins might be fun if you have along a friend with a good sense of humor.

Perverted Twilight Zone Rings of Hell in Dante's Inferno

My father tells the neurologist that on the drive over he saw a conga line of cobras undulating along the sidewalk. A severed sheep's head in bed with him the night before. His hallucinations, he says, are perverted Twilight Zone rings of Hell in Dante's *Inferno*—sexual, spiritual, mystical, and rife with horror.

Mary has had the tubes from her lungs removed but is still on oxygen. And my dad is actually a lot more functional now that they're back together. The neurologist says they've both survived this long, so well and against all odds, because they have each other.

They still kiss every time they are in the same room. He still calls her his girlfriend. Her plan is to get off oxygen and become his primary caretaker again. Last week we were all certain she was on her deathbed and this week she's taking over the world.

While sobbing with my therapist on Monday, I thought how opposite my mothers are, the first and last wives of my dad. One led by emotion, the other led by her head whose cracks are very hard to find. I want to be more stoic, more in control, more in charge, but it seems unlikely for me.

Root

In Reiki, I learn that the root chakra is home, at the base of the spine between our legs in our deepest center. The root chakra is blood red. It is connected to the adrenals. I burned out an adrenal gland many years ago and had to get it cut out. When I drive between home and the hospital I pray for my root chakra, I place one hand between my thighs. I pray, I hope to heal.

Breathe

Mary is on 24-hour oxygen now which reminds me to breathe. She seems to have no fear of death, she is simply preparing for it as one would for an important visitor. She's getting all of her affairs in order. She wants everything arranged in the house just so, everything accounted for.

Her primary concern is for my dad. The only time I see true pain on her face is when we talk about him. *Do you think you and Stan and Henry could move in here after I die?* she whispers. We're sitting on the couch. Her breathing is labored. She thinks she has a hernia from coughing but she can't have surgery because the doctor says it will not heal.

I'll think about it, I promise but I've thought about it already. The 12 days my Dad lived with us in September made my decision painfully clear. He is far too much for us to handle. He fell in the living room, he needed help in the shower. His medications alone were a logistical nightmare I couldn't continue to solve. Every day was exhausting and in the end, I remember thinking that this was a choice between his life and my own life. In the end, it's not a real choice. It just comes down to how I tell them and what we do instead.

Showing Up

Right now it's all about showing up. Showing up for myself, for my family, for my class. Showing up for birthday celebrations, death conversations, commitments, and responsibilities. Right now it's about getting out of bed, getting dressed, and fully inhabiting my day rather than creeping around the dark edges of it. Right now there's no way to face life except face first and head-on.

This week Mary enters hospice and I take my dad to visit a memory care facility. This week Matt, Mary's oldest son, turns 48 and a family friend creates a wonderful party for him with balloons and kazoos and colored party hats with chin straps and everything. We take videos and photos and record our voices and tell silly stories and live in the moment, knowing that soon—when Mary is gone— these moments will be gone with her.

Right now I feel a calm center of agency deep inside—a surprise for the girl who moved from one state to the next to outrun jobs and men, ran out on bar tabs, hid from bills, and turned her back on friends— was no one that anyone could count on. Now I'm handling power of attorney, passwords, keys, checkbooks, and bank accounts. Now it's time for me to show up and receive all of these good and bad and tangled, beautiful, terrible gifts life is giving me.

Running the Show

Last night Mary told me she wants to get through all of the late winter and spring birthdays and my trip to Mexico before she dies. She's planning for it sometime in April. At this point, I believe her. Her will is so strong. She's practically crawling across the floor to give my dad eye drops four times a day after his cataract surgery. She can barely walk or talk but she is still in steadfast control, running the show. Last night she asked me to fire the nurse I had tried so hard to hire because she has been a complete fiasco and Mary's frankly doing a better job on her own.

Yesterday I met with my dad's therapist. *One of two things is going to happen to your dad when he gets put in a home*, Dr. Weiner said to me. *Either a) he will die quickly or b) the old ladies will be all over him and he'll get a few girlfriends. He is still a gorgeous man!*

As if I hadn't thought of that, Dr. Weiner. As if I hadn't already thought of that.

Porous

Right now every phone call makes me jump. Every phone call makes Stan jump, too. Mary has entered hospice. She is on morphine. She's pared down to skin, bones, hair, and her radiant smile and shiny brown eyes but barely any flesh to hold onto.

I flag down the hospice nurse in the driveway. *A few days to a couple of weeks*, she says before I even ask. This week the official handover of paperwork takes place. I am now the keeper of the passwords and bank accounts and taxes and checkbooks. All the decisions to come. My dad—how will I hold his grief and his confusion? Do I have to? Can I create a buffer with my own boundaries? He'd die if he thought he was a burden to me.

I want to do everything I can but my skin is so porous, soaks in his emotions so intensely. It's easier to build a force field around those who aren't blood. Yesterday I had another massage with my hot massage therapist and thought I was going to die. I wanted to sob on the table and I wanted to turn over and pull him down on top of me and make him hold me forever and I wanted to get up and grab my clothes and run. Mostly I never wanted it to end.

Transfer of Power

Right now I'm trying to integrate the paperwork of two households without turning into a Kafka character. The transfer of bank accounts and bills and taxes has begun, and I'm trying not to let the sheer volume overwhelm me or take me down. Yesterday after a good 6 hours of transferring deeds, paying bills, and going on visits to memory care facilities, I came home and got in bed at 6:30 then stayed there the rest of the night.

Stan and Henry brought me pizza in bed. They came in to play guitar and watch TV shows and Henry had a full-on Teen Activist Group meeting with all his friends but I didn't get out of bed again. Mary has made it very clear she has no intention of dying within the hospice nurse's speculated time frame. The transfer of dad's property in the mountain to my name may have been a huge mistake but no one knows because the elder care lawyer just died. We are all hysterical over that.

Dad keeps accidentally tripping over the tubes from Mary's oxygen tank, unplugging it, making it impossible for her to breathe. Stan says I make sad, crushed, whimpering sounds in my sleep and that it is heartbreaking to hear. *Usually, you laugh in your sleep,* he says. *I do?* I said. *Yeah, you're never quiet,* he said. And I believe that.

Saint Mary

I started calling my stepmother *Saint Mary* years ago when my dad was first diagnosed with Lewy Body Dementia with Parkinson's disease. She had the unflappable tenacity to get him a proper diagnosis at Johns Hopkins when the neurologists in Richmond's medical community couldn't come up with anything better than *temporary psychosis*. Plus, she worked at St. Mary's in Human Resources. She never loses her temper, her patience never waivers. *Saint Mary.*

This week, as I was writing about Mary, I realized the most remarkable thing. She met and married my father when I was 12. She saw me through my awkward years, my drunken years, my drug years, my sleeping around years, my bad fashion and poorly applied make-up years, and she never once—not once—criticized me. For anything. I cannot remember an unkind word, judgment, unsolicited advice, or raised voice the entire time I've known her. She didn't ask me to call her *mom* like my first stepmother did. She never tried to run interference in my relationship with my dad or step into the shoes of my mother. She always let me be exactly who I was.

Mary and my dad have always been crazy about each other. Sometimes they bat their eyelids at each other like they are the only people in the room. Yesterday I sat for a few minutes on the side of her bed. I shared my astonishing revelation with her and breathing in as much air as she could, she whispered, *nothing to criticize.*

My eyes filled with tears. Can you imagine a bigger gift than that?

She's only criticized me 30 or 40 times, my dad said and we laughed. Everyone knows Mary likes to dress him, that his t-shirt and shorts wardrobe is not actually suitable for every occasion. *Mary, I think you're paving the way to heaven for the rest of us,* I said. *You're going first to make sure all the paperwork gets done for the rest of us.* We laughed again. Unlike the rest of us, she knows how to get shit done. *I'll do you right,* she said and we knew that to be true.

She'll do us right.

The Dying Time

In the dying time, time slows down. Everything, *every thing* is sacred. Every thing is significant. Each breath is a count away from the last. In the dying time, the sacred and the profane walk hand in hand. What were her last words? Did we get the password for her phone? Did she hear us sing? Did she hear the things we didn't say? What will we do with all these swabs and tubes? What did her parents look like when she saw a vision of them in the room? Who will wear her clothes? Who will wear her shoes? Who will wear her wedding ring?

Do you want to be in the room when they come to carry her away?

Everyone says goodbye in a different way. My son wears a suit and a bow tie and plays songs for her on his guitar. He knows she likes it when people dress up. Her sisters sing childhood songs. My father whispers in her ear. Her sons sleep on the floor and hold vigil the last night she is alive. Her beautiful friend, the hospice nurse, checks her pulse, heartbeat, breath. We each give her permission to go, in our own way.

The dying time is holy holy holy and as part of life, as ordinary as air.

The Day After

The day after Mary dies, my dad says, Valley, *I just want you to know I'll be getting married again, and soon. That's just the way I am.* I've moved into the rental house with him and we are together all the time now. Mary was his third wife and they were married for 31 years. He adored her and she, him. They never stopped being newlyweds. On her deathbed, he kissed her cheek and said *you're still my soulmate and you always will be, Mary Pierce, my love.*

But, in addition to wanting to marry again, my dad has wanted to start drinking, smoking, and doing drugs, too. Lately, we've started losing track of what prescription drugs he's been taking and when. One morning he calls me into his room just after 6 AM. I haven't had my coffee yet when he dumps a film canister of pot onto his dresser top.

Can you make a cookie for me? he asks.

I don't know how, Dad, I say.

Oh, I'm sure you could figure it out, he says.

Dad, actually with my sobriety I can't.

Oh my God, I forgot! I'm so sorry, he says.

Later that day he makes the pot cookie himself.

When Everything Falls Apart

This week I pick up Mary's ashes and place them in the wooden box made by her son from her parent's dining room table. I provide death certificates to the bank, the insurance company, credit cards, and Social Security. I take my dad for a haircut and a straight razor shave. We have a memorial service, Valentine's Day, and a birthday party. We look at a thousand old pictures, tracing our shared and separate pasts. I hear him weeping beside me and from all the way across the house.

And now, after the 8th day in his guest room, I am vacillating between the hopeful relief and utter heartbreak of finding the next home for my dad. A memory care center, a fenced-in community. Somewhere safe. It feels like trapping a lion, like taking a wild majestic beast and pacing out the square footage of his cage.

It feels like betrayal.

My dad would like to live alone in the country with a tool shed and huge bonfires and uncrowded acres where he can continue to carve sculptures and expand into the world around him.

But, he's started falling and I'm not strong enough to lift him up. Sometimes he forgets how to spell his own name. He gets lost inside a pullover shirt. Cell phones and remote controls are foreign objects from foreign lands. There are portals to other worlds under the kitchen sink, men with hooves in the parking lot, a whole host of wildlife I cannot see galloping through this house.

Some grief is simple. You miss your loved one. It is inconceivable that they are gone. Your grief is beautiful and pure. It's different from grieving for someone who is still right in front of you.

My father tells me he's in the midst of a catastrophe. He's lost his home and his profession and his wife and his cat. I can't argue. He says everything is falling apart, but that it must be coming together, too, because life is an infinity symbol. With every contraction, expansion. He says, if you don't know where you are going, any road will take you there. I keep doing the next right thing in front of me to do. Feeling it out, blind, throwing myself forward into the day.

The Bureaucracy of Grief

This week I have lost a set of keys, my medicine bag, my sunglasses, my phone. I've missed appointments and found myself forgetting what I was going to say or why I was going to say it. You have grief brain, friends tell me. I'm in survival mode

My dad has lost everything he's ever cared about. I'm helping him settle into a life he never dreamed he'd have to face on his own. Sitting down to the page feels less like a practice and more like triage. It doesn't feel like tending to the root of the original wound— it feels like pulling it out of the ground with my own two hands.

I'm forwarding mail, amending rental agreements, signing checks. And there's still so much paperwork to do, so many objects to re-home. I have felt despair and anguish. There have been huge unbridled swaths of grace. I have felt carried and protected. I've come face to face with the bureaucracy of grief. Every stage of the ritual of death comes with a new form to fill out.

Every day my dad discovers something he needs that he's left behind. I drive the route between his old home and the memory care unit 100 times. Now his doctor's notes come to me.

Degenerative discs, Parkinson's, neurological disease. I feel like I'm trying to gather pieces of plaster after an explosion to rebuild a home.

In memory care, my dad likes chair Tai Chi, pet therapy, and singing. The caregivers are kind but the conversations between the residents at dinner are full of non-sequiturs. Every day my dad has wild hallucinations and cries alone in his room. I walk the line between caregiver, daughter, and my own true self.

Bedlam

My dad was a social worker before he went into carpentry. He worked with troubled youth, senior citizens, and in a forensic psychiatry ward. His patients were the bedtime stories of my youth.

The nurses at my dad's new facility say he reminds them of a social worker still. He says things like *don't let your mood go down with the sun* and the Isak Dinesen quote, *The cure for anything is saltwater— sweat, tears, or the sea.*

He calls me before 7 am to tell me there were people screaming and banging on the walls of his room all night. The nurses came into his room scolding him and carrying babies. I race to the center, crying the whole way, and sitting on the side of the bed he says, *But come to think of it these things happen at home, too.*

He says he feels like he's in a college dorm, a correctional facility. He says he feels like he's in Bedlam. As I walk with him through the halls, a woman screams *I HATE YOU MOTHER* again and again. My heart wrenches like a wet sponge. She's trapped in a nightmare and now it seems, so is he.

Last night after a 20-minute phone call with a med tech, I discover that his primary care physician has written his med list wrong. I want to scream with rage. I want to slam heads. I'm rarely violent but I feel violent now. Can't they see that this is my *Dad*?

Over the last few weeks, I have felt folded in a bubble wrap of grace. I have felt God's hand holding me up. I have also felt terror, heartache, and despair. I'm trying to forgive human error. I'm trying to forgive the dementia invading my father's brain. I'm trying to forgive the new place he has to live away from his beloved farm. But I'm not at the acceptance stage yet.

New Home

As we walk around the grounds of his new home, in the cold gray, my dad tells me he joined a singing class and that it was fun. *What made it fun?* I ask.

Giving up trying to be cool, he says. My father has never joined any group activities and the number of classes he's taken so far amazes me. The woman who screamed *I HATE YOU, MOTHER* all day yesterday started singing West Virginia folk songs and calling him Tommy today.

She is Mommy Dearest meets Mrs. Godzilla, he tells me. The first time I saw her she was yelling *GET OUT OF MY LIFE* at a care partner. There's so much to process with all of this newness. The home feels like a gift from God compared to everywhere else we looked at, but it's still a hard gift to accept. The umbilical cord I feel stretched between me and my dad is ages old. I am the bounce of his reflection, the consequence of his personality, the recipient of his addiction to love, sex, drugs, drinking, and adventure into the big blue wild.

It's weird for it to be the two of us together again, the way I dreamed it would be when I was seven and asked him to marry me in the Safeway on Grace Street.

Moving Through

When we visit Dad on Sunday he tells us about a terrific fight two old ladies had with each other—screaming all kinds of foul curses—and he laughs and laughs, shoulders bobbing up and down. I am so grateful that this time it is funny instead of sinister, ridiculous rather than alarming, less of a nightmare, less sad than the initial few weeks of transfer trauma and shock.

Dad told me he thought he had suffered the worst grief a human could suffer when their dog Shelby died several summers ago. He hadn't known it could still get so much worse. My stepbrother says his heart breaks every time he steps into the space they once occupied. It causes great difficulty packing up the rental house but we are moving through.

Passports and Plane Tickets

We have our passports and our plane tickets. We have shuttle buses and Airbnbs and we're nearly ready for our boarding passes. In two weeks I will fly to Mexico, my first trip out of the country in 23 years. There are so many reasons I haven't traveled before and so many reasons I'm ready to now.

I drank, hitchhiked, and did reckless things with strange men all the way across Europe. When I got sober at 23, I didn't think I could leave the USA without becoming that same girl again. It's taken a long period of healing to make me think otherwise. Watching Mary die and taking over the affairs of my dad has shown me there are lots of things I can do that I never thought I could. We are preparing to put our house on the market. I am studying Reiki and shamanism and collaborating with a fabulous artist to lead a retreat in Mexico. My dreams are coming true.

Meanwhile, new letters and forms and subscriptions to be canceled appear in the mail every day. Yesterday I canceled a dentist appointment Mary had coming up soon. The day before that, I finished her life insurance claim and sent it off in the mail. My stepbrothers and husband and I have been trying to generate a comprehensive plan for moving the rest of their stuff out. Filing cabinets, work histories, boxes of photo albums and scrapbooks and old letters and sculptures and plants and walls and walls of art. It's not the furniture or the lamps or china that get me, it's the intimate collections of family lore, the stuff we couldn't sell but I don't see how I can possibly keep. How do you dismantle a home you somehow thought would exist forever?

Dad, meanwhile, is settling into his new surroundings but he still doesn't fully understand why he can't get up and drive away or live completely on his own. This is one of the parts that hurts most. My therapist tells me I am responsible for keeping him safe, not for taking away his grief or protecting him from his pain. Taking that in is the hardest of all.

You Are Going to Mexico

I arrive in San Miguel at night after two flights and a two-hour shuttle. Along the highways and through town it's all cacti and goats and cows and horses and so many wandering dogs, women selling pineapples, and food trucks on the side of the road that make me want to throw myself out of the van to gobble up their wares.

This is the longest I've been away from home since I moved back two decades ago, the biggest trip I've taken sober. And I'm here to lead a retreat with eight beautiful women. I didn't think I could travel without drinking or getting high or sleeping with men I met on public transportation.

It's a wonderful surprise to find what a country looks, sounds, feels, and tastes like without my senses blurred—to be the bride of wonder rather than the bride of scary men and addiction.

My loft at the Airbnb is full of deep rich blues, ochres, yellows. I feel like I'm in a blood orange studded with turquoise. The garden is magnificent, the rooftop is insane. The view of the city is to die for.

I cannot believe I have this place to myself for a full week and then a week more with my family. Two weeks sounds like two lifetimes. I do miss Stan and Henry and the pets. I do wish they were all with me but solitude is part of this vision quest. I buy a plastic cup of flan from a woman who has opened up the front door of her house with all kinds of delicious and brightly colored wonders. The flan is delicious like a cinnamon cream pudding. I have no food in the house except—thank God—coffee, and Linda, my co-teacher, was so sweet to bring me chocolate pistachio biscotti, so coffee and dessert for breakfast!

I'm on the rooftop now and my senses are inundated with hot air balloons and church bells and dogs barking, and birds and church towers and huge purple trees. My building is full of statues of Buddha and lions and mermaids and eagles and angels. I can hear trucks barreling by on the narrow cobblestone streets. The sun coming over the mountain looks like a tremendous golden mane. My soul has been starving for this.

I feel like this trip was planned by someone with a better calendar than me, a trip that for months I didn't know if I'd be able to take, the refrain of my therapist replaying in my ears over and over. *You are going to Mexico, you are going to Mexico, you are, you are, even if the world falls apart around you, you are going, you are going, you are going to Mexico. Even if everyone dies, they will still be dead when you get back!*

And so right now I am here. I am free. I'm in love with the coffee and mangoes and refried beans, the triumphant chorus of birds and beeping horns, the music of dogs and cats, and fireworks that keep me company all night long.

A Valley All My Own

When the retreat is over, I meet a man named Alejandro. Alejandro is tall and handsome with charcoal black hair and green-blue eyes. He is half Mexican and half American with a low resonant voice and quiet strength in his mouth and eyes. I've hired Alejandro to be my spiritual guide for 2 1/2 hours. He takes me through a meditation that opens a door to a room I'd slammed shut tight.

I let myself fall apart, weep, truly embody my session. I do not hold onto beauty or dignity or being cool. I blow my nose and let tears run hot down my red face. During the meditation he asks me questions and I begin to truly listen to myself. I walk through jungles and mountains and oceans with horses and buffalo and I climb high into the night sky. I tell Alejandro my feelings are too big for my body and he encourages me, again and again, to simply feel and surrender. I do not abandon my life even though I fall completely in love, eyes, heart, ears. All of my senses are lit up with mountains in every direction. I'm cradled in a valley all my own.

Matriarch

On Monday night we have a birthday dinner for my stepbrother who is turning 49. Ever since Mary died, all family occasions have been celebrated at our new house, moving me into a matriarchal position which I am mostly ready for. It feels like a great honor and a great responsibility. My stepbrothers are both covered in tattoos and on Monday night they tell amazing stories about times they've lived out of their cars in different states.

They are fantastic uncles to my son who loves them but is more mature than they are. At the birthday party, my dad gives my stepbrother a roll of duct tape stuffed into a sock in a Christmas container I've given him with his name still on it. Mary's brother-in-law and dad both have Parkinson's with fairly intense tremors so the table looks like the scene of a friendly food fight and we all sing happy birthday with great joy, if completely out of key.

While Those We Love Die

The day before the first anniversary of Mary's death, I get a call from the home that my dad blacked out and fell off the activity bus. He is fine, but I returned to my seat at the table of the writing class I was teaching feeling as if I had one less layer of skin.

My helplessness around my dad's disease, the disbelief that my beautiful stepmother died at only 69, the reality of living while those we love die. I would drown in the ocean of feeling if I didn't keep bailing water out onto the page, which I did that morning. I'm infinitely grateful that in my work I don't have to pretend everything is fine if it isn't, that I can let the truth be what it is.

And the truth is that my life has never been better. I have things I didn't even know I wanted or in some cases definitely did not want. Sobriety, a home, a car, a committed relationship, good work, serenity, happiness, joy, a sunroom, a ninth-grader, a meditation practice, two cats, a dog, a bearded dragon, amazing friends, health insurance. Even though I spent years actively trying to destroy it, I live a charmed and miraculous life.

The Multiverse

This morning on the elliptical I began a *This American Life* episode called *the Branching Gardens of the Universe* about quantum theory and alternate realities and how after each decision we make, another universe is created by the decision we did not make. I know none of this is new but I'm thinking of my father who often tells me he has left this dimension and entered another one, that he inhabits a multiverse, that there are lives and spirits transposed over what we see all around us.

It's fascinating but just yesterday I started to feel afraid that I may get swept up and into his world and not be able to get out. Who knows what happens to daughters who spend too much time in proximity to tears in the time-space continuum?

I've spent the last 18 months practicing energetic healing and I can feel the subtle shifts that happen inside me, the flashes of insight, the heat, and energy. But it's hard for me to know the impact on other people, what happens when my energy field interacts with theirs. I'm learning about this now, the science behind the feeling and it is mind-blowing and exciting in this universe for me.

What God Looks Like

On Monday I make lasagna and pick my dad up from the home. Instead of buying new plates for our new house, we are using my grandmother's china. If they don't survive the dishwasher, to hell with them, they aren't doing anyone any good in the attic. My dad points out the formation of clouds on the delicate old red and white dinner plates and tells us that growing up he thought God's face was in the clouds. *That's what God looked like to me!* He says and then he holds his arms up like Jesus and says, *Holy shit, man!* and we all laugh so hard.

After lasagna and pumpkin pie we go see my mom's performance at the completion of her first comedy improv class. We buy her an enormous bouquet of flowers and arrive early. I feel like a mom to my mom. I am so excited and nervous for her—awed and proud but also terrified. I'm amazed at what she can and will do.

Ninety minutes later we are all clapping and laughing until we nearly cry. *That really took balls!* my Dad says and for a moment when he hugs my Mom I can see 40 years collapse between them, any anger or betrayal or bitterness gone. Only love left.

The Language of Art

My dad has started to draw. He's disinterested in the crafts offered in memory care and is no longer allowed to operate power tools for carving sculptures. He's made quite a collection of massive and surreal figures out of wood and old machinery that look like they come from his dreams. His drawings are more like scribbles. Wild, effusive, complicated scribbles. At a glance you can't tell if they were created by a genius or a madman—or both. Initially you want to respond as you would to a child or maybe an elephant who learned to paint with her trunk. But then you look a little closer and a little longer, and he explains them to you, and you begin to see what he sees climbing out of the depths.

Dad calls me to ask if I have a paper cutter. He wants to prepare his drawings as gifts for the holidays. *I do have a paper cutter!* I exclaim. *And we can go to AC MOORE to look at frames.* I've just learned this morning that AC MOORE is closing and my grief is a lot like actual grief—shock, abandonment, bargaining. I'm a terrible crafter but the idea of crafts always cheers me up. As we enter the store, the Yankee candles have already taken on the Scent of Despair, and clerks and customers alike are wondering where they will go next. I lay all of Dad's drawings on the counter and started hauling over frames. *Oh, we can't use glass,* my Dad says. *We are going to be mailing these.*

My mom is an artist and comes over one night to help with matting. As she sorts his art and I scotch-tape fronts to backs, I wonder when was the last time the three of us were alone in a room together? Forty-two years after the end of their marriage, they are separate entities. They are fascinating and complex in completely different ways. Tonight I see their perfect convergence through the language of art.

Mom holds up a piece and describes what she saw—a bird, an angel—and Dad says no, that's a metal structure collapsing in a run-down mall. Mom and I take turns gently steering Dad back on track as we make our way through the stack of surreal mind-scapes that he would describe in great detail. *Vietnamese Girl Making a Decision at 7-11. Airplane Crashing into the Face of a Man. A Lonely Soldier Living Out His Days Guarding a Railroad Track with No Railroad.*

Dad says maybe so-and-so won't really appreciate this menacing dark blob called *Boy Removing His Intestines in Columbus, Ohio,* and I suggest cutting out a Norman Rockwell print and pasting it into the mat instead. And then we all laugh and keep going. Both of my parents taught me that. You make art out of life because your life depends on it. Even if no one likes it. Even if you lose your memory or your tools or the security of benefits and a full-time job. Even if all you have is a ballpoint pen.

Quantum Mechanics

My stepsister, Llewellyn, comes over to help me curate the art show we are hosting for my father. I'm so grateful he had the brilliant idea of hiring her—I would collapse under the weight of so much work, framing and cataloging. Before Llewellyn arrives, Dad stands at my dining room window, laughing. *Look at the short man in the beaver costume playing the banjo in your neighbors' backyard!* he exclaims. I see the barrel on the neighbors' deck and know just what he means. I laugh, too.

Often my dad's hallucinations are bizarre and hilarious. Often, but not always. For the last few months, he's been terrified that a drunk construction worker is going to move in below him and keep him up all night with nefarious shouting. Dad has visions of Hell and War and the Dead, but it's rednecks he fears most.

After Llewellyn arrives, we sort through his artwork and interview him about his artistic process for the introduction to a book of his drawings. She calmly helps us figure out what needs to be done next, a task that has begun to seem insurmountable to me through the lens of dad's confusion. It's real work—hard work—to separate out what is true from Dad's liquid, reflected version of reality.

A few nights ago, Stan dreamed my father died and it's like I'm standing in a field looking into the middle distance where one of two equally impossible outcomes will occur. My dad will die or he will continue to live, becoming further gone. Death by a thousand cuts. I cannot imagine his death but it's also painful to imagine the rest of his life. Over lunch, I ask Henry who he thinks I am more like, my mother or father. *I don't mean to be morbid,* Henry says, *but I don't know what Papa is really like.*

Oh yes, you do, I say. And after a moment, I say, *You're right, you don't.* Henry has never known the sharp, tidy, efficient, capable man my dad was.

Dad moves seamlessly in and out of alternate realities, and the more I read about quantum mechanics and shamanism, the less I dismiss what he tells me about the other side. But we live on this Earth in this timeline, one that marks him as a flight risk who needs a locked care facility. I feel afraid of losing him entirely to the other side but equally afraid that I might follow him—now or eventually— through genetics or magnetism.

Spirit World

Last night I dreamed that Mary figured out how to contact us from the spirit world through a fax machine. She figured out the number to dial, knowing I wouldn't pick up an area code I didn't recognize and she'd planned out a detailed, typed message that was translated through her voice. I can still hear her voice from the dream, self-assured, practical, confident, and kind, but I can't remember anything she said.

Last night we picked my dad up for pizza and he talked about how much he misses her, and how it's impossible to believe she's not here. It's like the year of her rapid decline and death, the sale of their house and all that has followed are nightmares to wake up from. I'm still processing my own disbelief. It's hard for me to wrap my head around it all and I don't have neurological damage and dementia. I can't imagine what it's like for him. So much of him is still intact. The original him isn't gone at all. What's new are the layers of reality plastered on top of this one.

Little Girl

On Monday as I prepare to pick my dad up for a weekly dinner I feel a fist rising through my stomach and as it clenches I have to sit back down again. Tears rush my eyes and my throat burns. I can't move in a sudden paralysis of feeling. Tim calls and I am crying so hard I almost can't speak. *Cancel,* he tells me. *Get off the phone with me, call your dad right now and cancel dinner. You're not going.* And so I don't go.

When Dad calls on Tuesday I feel a stab of tenderness for him so sharp my chest hurts, but I don't go pick him up then either. Maybe Thursday night I tell myself. Maybe by Thursday night, I'll be ready. I have never said no to my dad. I've never canceled. I have never not shown up. I've been a good daughter.

No, the anger and hurt have been tucked away. Until now. They are seeping out. They're spreading like spilled blood or poison.

Thank God I had Mary for 30 years stabilizing and buffering my dad's sometimes tenuous connection with reality. From 13 to 43 I had a dad who had a stable and loving wife. He still never disciplined me, never said no, never set boundaries. He stoked the fires of my insatiable need to feel special every time I saw him but I was safe. Safe to worship my heroic perfect dad.

Unfortunately, there were those 12 to 13 years of childhood development before that. The dad in rehab and relapse—moving, hitch-hiking, getting high. The revolving doors for various beautiful women all of whom I hated and at least one of whom was violently jealous of me.

I've been having a rough time over my dad's absence in therapy, anger and rage rising to the surface. I know he never intended to hurt me and this is where it's so confusing. How can what felt so good hurt so bad? How can a man who meant me no harm have fucked up so much? How do I take care of myself and him, moving forward? The books I read say I will heal. I was the chosen one, the companion, his partner and confidante, his little wife. The books say that I will learn how to reset, adjust my boundaries, restructure relationships, to find my right size with him and with me.

By Thursday I am an adult again. I can pick my dad up from memory care, fix dinner, buy him shoes, and a raincoat on Amazon, take him back home feeling a calm steady love. This is my definition of a miracle. Being able to care for and repair the inner little girl while being an adult in this world.

March 11, 2020

Right now I am feeling my first edge of panic in the face of the pandemic. I got a call this morning from the memory care center that my dad is under quarantine for at least five days due to a stomach virus. But is it really a stomach virus they are quarantining for? Thank God thank God, thank God, I had him over for dinner Thursday night before the world shut down.

Tim, who is closely following the news, thinks probably not. He thinks they're trying to limit panic and the timing is just too coincidental. I don't know. I do know I felt the cold icicle of fear and a hot wave of grief slice through my rib cage. As complicated as my feelings have been about him recently, the thought of him under lockdown, cut off from friends and family breaks my heart in two. Everyone wears the cloak of fear and the unknown differently and until about an hour ago, mine was loose.

Chicken Little

My dad is on lockdown for God knows how long and I think his mental state must be very close to sheer hell. He has a fever, diarrhea, vomiting, and body aches along with anxiety, panic and not fully understanding what the hell is going on.

Yesterday he called to ask if I could return a pair of pants I ordered for him on Amazon. *The pants can wait, Dad,* I kept saying. *The pants can wait.*

Right now the truth is that everything is fine. Just fine. In my house, we have food and an internet connection. My kid is old enough to pretty much self-govern. My husband hasn't quit working yet though every day he wonders if he should. I have a mile-high stack of library books and art projects and a dog to walk and a nice neighborhood to walk her in. But. It's the Buts. The buts and what if's of the future. For me and everyone. For my dad.

Money, resources, connection, sanity. Mental health, spiritual fitness. The biggest part of me believes I've had a life of training and therapy in recovery and meditation to prepare for this. The other part is running around like Chicken Little yelling, *The sky is falling, the sky is falling down.*

Tiny Raft on a Big Sea

My dad calls at 3:45 AM to tell me he's been stranded naked in Portsmouth again. Last time it was Petersburg. He was divided in half, unable to feel whole. *Oh, Dad,* I say. *I'm so sorry. Can you go talk to one of the nurses outside of your room?*

Yes, he says. *I'm so sorry to do this to you, Valley.*

It's OK, Dad, I say. *It's OK.* I toss and turn and cry and finally sleep again.

I practice self-care like it's a mandate to keep my own monsters and demons at bay: rage, pettiness, self-centered fear, vindictiveness, hostility, keeping score. I don't recite words by rote, I throw in my whole body weight when I pray.

I climb into my little raft on the big sea and try not to let the waves crash over the sides. I try not to pierce the rubber of the raft, or rock too hard from side to side. I try to follow the narrow trajectory of gratitude and sanity and structure, a new route on these big and stormy waves. I cast out lines to drag up sunken treasure, and at last, the gratitude rises up and crashes over me huge and real and my tiny raft becomes a mighty ship at sea.

The Trial

My dad calls for the fourth time in a row in the middle of the night. The tribunal is meeting right outside his door, he tells me. It is like a trial or a ceremony but he can't understand the words they are saying.

Did you talk? I ask.

Oh no, he says. *That would be inappropriate.* Then he hears the redneck man with a gun shouting. *He might shoot me soon,* my dad tells me, and then there is gospel music and voodoo way down deep in the Bayou. And he holds the phone out so I can hear it, too. I hear a clatter, bump, the sound of his hand thumping against the body of the phone, and then quiet and then nothing.

Do you feel safe? I ask.

Not especially, he says.

Can you sleep tonight? I ask.

I think so, he says.

Try to get some sleep, Dad, I said, *and we will do everything we can to make you safe.*

Thank you Valley, he says. *Thank you for everything you do.*

But what can I do? What can I do other than what I have done? He tells me they've given him an enema, that he has lockjaw, that there's an open wound on his back, that the nurses are children and they're mean. I make calls. I pray. I detach. I try to find out as best I am capable of what is true, what's just in his head, and if there's a difference.

Mother's Day

On Saturday my dad's memory care center hosts a Mother's Day parade. I've known about it for weeks but the truth of it didn't hit me until the morning of and then it felt like the earth had cracked in two and I was being asked to jump over a vast divide. Oh shit oh shit oh shit. I'm going to see my dad. I wrapped the gifts we were dropping off and Henry drew *Happy Mother's Day Papa* on a huge poster board.

Isn't this going to be kind of like driving through a zoo and looking at the old people in cages, my mother asks, and I say, *Yes it's weird as hell but what else are we going to do?* And as our car creeps closer to the line of old people in wheelchairs and lawn chairs behind the fence line I feel the sadness and guilt that have been shoved down, geyser up and out.

And though I am a huge advocate for crying to heal I do everything I can not to outright sob as we wave at my dad through the window and then keep driving by. His face is confused before registering ours, and then it lights up into a huge brilliant smile. The stories

I've told myself to make this OK fall apart, and I sob hard as we turn the corner behind other cars waving to loved ones they can't touch or hold.

Why doesn't he live with us? I wonder again and it's like sometimes all the answers I know to that question fly out the window, get trapped in blackness and all I can feel is that I abandoned my father, consigned him to an institution, the kind he once told me he'd rather die than live in. The guilt makes me gasp for breath and reason is gone and I'm just a little girl again missing and longing for her dad. I need to write out the reasons why and tape them up everywhere. I need to keep that part of my sanity intact.

Insane Scenarios

I talk to my Dad every other day or so. Can you imagine being on lockdown in a building full of dementia patients during a pandemic when you're hallucinating all kinds of insane scenarios layered on top of the real insane scenarios? Me neither. Not being able to see or save my dad has forced a level of surrender I could not previously achieve. I'm having trouble finding surrender on my own. Surrender to the truth that the only person's happiness or well-being I can help is mine alone.

My dad calls me to update me on the rednecks in the basement of his memory care center. *I've learned the drunk redneck dad is actually just an actor,* my dad says. *And I told him a joke to change our power dynamic. You have to be careful how you use power, he warned, but humor is usually a pretty safe way to do it.*

What was the joke, dad? I ask.

That cauliflower is just broccoli in a dress, dad says and we laugh. The brain is so amazing. It's both the source of such intense suffering and the antidote to that suffering simultaneously.

I feel like my Dad is the madwoman in Mr. Rochester's attic that Jane Eyre hears thumping around in the night. He's a burr in my heart that I'm building a callous around because what good does it do me to feel his pain right now? His phone calls are unsettling and sad, his connection to reality just solid enough to let the horror in, but too porous to keep the horror out.

There's No Accounting for the Strangeness of Things

Stories from the psychiatric hospital where my father worked became my bedtime stories when I was little. Once, as my father was completing his morning rounds, he found one of his patients lying in his bathtub, hands clutching a single fake red rose, arms crossed over his chest, a perfect portrait of death. *Are you OK, Mr. Johnson?* my Dad asked.

Mr. Johnson bolted straight upright in his bathtub, looked at my dad, and said, *There's no accounting for the strangeness of things.* This has been one of my dad's favorite sayings ever since. In fact, he chose it as the title for his show of recent artwork.

My dad has always been a man who blends poetry and dreams and fantasies with memories and hallucinations, all of which sound equally plausible and equally absurd, like being in a house of mirrors where the walls stand an equal chance of offering escape, or prison. And now, looping back through time, the past is the future, and the future is the present.

Peruvian Dictator

Sunday I get a call that my dad fell and had a seizure and was unresponsive for a period of time so they sent him by ambulance to the ER at Saint Mary's. I am able to see him there after they take his vitals. It is the first time I've been in the room with him in three months. My frozen heart starts to thaw and gush out in a flood. When I arrive in the ER a nurse asks if I am the daughter from Peru.

Probably, I say. Dad explained to them that his daughter was living in South America dating a Peruvian dictator and that just that morning he had given a speech for the revolution. *It was just like Woody Allen's* Bananas, he tells me, and we laugh hard. It is so good to see him and when they make me leave, my sobs fog up my glasses. I can't gulp in air and breathe behind my mask so I have to sit on a curb and cry before I can get to my car in the parking lot.

It is like leaving a sick child behind in the care of strangers. He doesn't know who they are or where he is but he knows me and he asks after Henry and Stan and all the animals. He tells me he knows the hallucinations are just hallucinations but that they are actually happening, too. The line between all things is so blurry. There is no certainty about anything anymore. And then they tell me to leave and not come back until they get his Covid test results.

Death Bed

I sit here, bedside. Breathing in every breath. Prepared but not ready, like a friend said. Never ready.

When the hospital chaplain asks my dad if he would like to pray, my dad says, *I would like to eat pie on a mountain top.* This sounds like the perfect prayer to me.

As I sit beside my father, I draw and write and read him poetry and play him songs and talk to him about all of the people who love him and all the stories we've lived. My heart shatters and fills back up with love again and again.

I whisper to him about his freedom, about the most amazing freedom he will ever feel, waiting for him on the other side, beyond this world, this room, this stark white bed, into the great Wild Beyond.

Goodbye

I play so many of the songs we loved. *Innocent When You Dream, Wondering Where the Liars Are, Hallelujah.* I play the Roches, Bob Dylan, Paul Simon, and the Rolling Stones. I tell him stories and jokes that he loved to tell me.

Shut up, he explained.

Shoot low boys, they're riding Shetland ponies!

I tell him all the things I loved about him and all the incredible memories we have. I forgive him his trespasses and I ask him to forgive mine. He can't form words anymore but he speaks with his eyes and I squeeze sponges of cold water onto his lips.

I wipe down his forehead, rub his feet. Hold up the phone when his sisters call so they can tell him goodbye. At one point the hospice nurse yells at me to go home. *You're not doing anyone any good here!* she says. He's not going to die today. *Go home and take a shower!*

I obey but rush back to the hospital as fast as I can with clean clothes to sleep in. I listen to books on tape and guided meditations and weep so hard and love so much I don't know what could possibly be left. When his breathing staggers and his eyes close I call my mom and Stan and Henry and they come and we sit in chairs around his bed and sing and laugh and cry together.

Henry plays *I'll Follow You Into the Dark* on his guitar and we stroke my dad's head, and hold his hand and say goodbye as he takes his last breath.

Mountains and Valleys

On Tuesday morning I put on the prettiest dress I can find and drive to the funeral home. A man standing out front wearing a suit and medical mask asks me if I am there for the service.

No, I tell him. *I'm here to pick someone up.* Inside, a woman in a mask hands me a white paper bag with a white cardboard box and six crisp white envelopes. A Certificate of Cremation and five Certificates of Death. The same funeral home told me earlier in the week I'd need special documentation to take my dad out of state. I'd noted that fact in my journal, even though I won't need it.

The bag is much heavier than I expect it to be. I clasp it to my chest and carry it like a baby, sobs rising and heaving in my throat. I have to sit in my car in the parking lot for a long time before I am ready to make the drive home.

I watched my father die three days ago. I'd held his hands, wiped his brow, sung him songs, told him how much I loved him, how much everyone loved him, and that it was OK to go. That he'd lived a big, wide open, and beautiful life and that his work here was one.

It was the most privileged and holy and devastating task I've ever carried out as a daughter. The steepest mountain we've climbed together. That night I stayed up as late as I could because that morning I'd still had a dad.

My stepbrother carves a beautiful chestnut box to hold my father's ashes. It sits on my altar by the fireplace between candles and flowers and incense and other sacred things. In the spring we make some pies and carry Mary and him up the mountain in the Blue Ridge near the Shenandoah Valley where he was born, where I was conceived, that I was named after, where we camped throughout my childhood, where he carved me bows and arrows, where his heart returned again and again.

We scatter their ashes among the trees and rocks and blueberry bushes on the land he loved so much, on the land where he'd started to build a home, a home where he thought he'd live forever. We help him complete his journey of the flesh while he's on a vast and eternal journey of the Spirit. And we won't even have to leave the state.

Valhalla

This week I've been shepherded along by grace. A swath of this grief has been infused with creativity. I feel run by it, like it's the spirit steering my bones. It's like colors, lines, shapes, ink, and paint can heal me. I can't stop drawing. Pencils and paint and markers and pens. Bears, horses, buffalo, crows, lions, all the animals in my mind begging to find life on the page. After three weeks of deep emotional hibernation, I'm cracking open stored up energy and inspiration. Loss can be alchemized, more than the sum of its parts. Creativity is the bridge between pain and healing. The best way I know to honor and synthesize death is through acts of creation.

Two years ago my dad told me he dreamed I was flying a rocket ship full of people over Mount Everest. He dreamed I came from Atlantis when I was four. He saw a comet shoot through space and hit the earth as I shot through space between my mother's legs.

My father and I had an unspoken don't ask, don't tell policy. He signed the report cards I wouldn't show my mom. He let me fight my own wars, wage my own battles. He trusted that if I fell, I would find a way back up again. I picture my dad feasting in the Great Hall with the Gods, shining down on me, guiding my pen.

A Brief and Fantastic Celebration of Life

This week I erupt into violent tears after glimpsing a shadow of a cataract in my dog's googly movie star eyes. It is an opaque crystal ball and in it, I see a reflection of her eventual death and our grief, and then my loved ones' deaths, and my death, too.

I am constantly aware of death. My immortality died this summer. Not to say I haven't always been able to feel grief and outrage and horror at murder, war, violence, police brutality, cancer— I have, I do. But death hovered in the abstract, just above my capacity to feel it.

Death is with me now as I slice a tomato, hammer a nail, sweep the floor. Death is with me as I draw, as I write, as I listen to the radio, and read the news. More murder, more virus, more suffering. And still, something coming up from a deep well within tells me to prepare the way forward, and armor my spirit with beauty.

I understood flowers for the first time the day my father died. I've always liked flowers just fine, of course. But when my friend Kristen bought me every single purple bouquet she could find at

Trader Joe's, those flowers returned me to the present in a way nothing else could.

Each bloom entirely itself, a small explosive miracle of intricate beauty. A way of anchoring ourselves to the core vitality of the earth, even as we walk together or alone, ever closer to death. A brief and fantastic celebration of life.

Colophon

There's No Accounting for the Strangeness of Things was typeset in Freight Text and Bagnard.

Freight Text is a serif typeface designed by Joshua Darden and published through GarageFonts in 2005. Freight is an extremely versatile superfamily with many different versions available, making it suitable for a wide range of typographic challenges. It is the type family used as part of the identity system for the National Museum of African American History and Culture in Washington D.C.

Bagnard Regular was inspired by the graffitis of an anonymous prisoner of the napoleonic wars. Bagnard was created by Sebastien Sanfilippo and is currently distributed by Love Letters.

There's No Accounting for the Strangeness of Things was designed by Llewellyn Hensley & Content–Aware Graphic Design — **content-aware.design.**

Thank you
for supporting *Unzipped*

Our project is made possible by readers like you. We are infinitely grateful to our patrons who make it possible for us to continue publishing urgent, brave, and true stories! To learn more about supporting us through our subscription program, our online litmag, classes, and workshops, visit **lifein10minutes.com/unzipped.** We would love to write, read, and (metaphorically) unzip with you.

CPSIA information can be obtained
at www.ICGtesting.com
Printed in the USA
LVHW031815241121
704369LV00014B/350